ARABIC EXPRESS: SPEAK LEBANESE

A COMPLETE COURSE

FREE AUDIO:
www.bernardkhoshaba.com

Coursebook–Workbook in one

Learn in the classroom (University, college, school)
Teach yourself (Learner friendly)

BERNARD KHOSHABA

Copyright © BERNARD KHOSHABA 2017

ALL RIGHTS RESERVED

No part of this publication may be reproduced, stored in a retrieval system, or transmitted in any form or by any means, electronic, mechanical, photocopying, recording or otherwise, without the prior written permission of the publisher.

First printed by Green Print Centre - UNSW

ISBN 978 0 9943270 2 4

Also by Bernard Khoshaba
'Arabic Express: A Complete Course in Spoken and Written Arabic.'

PHOENICIA

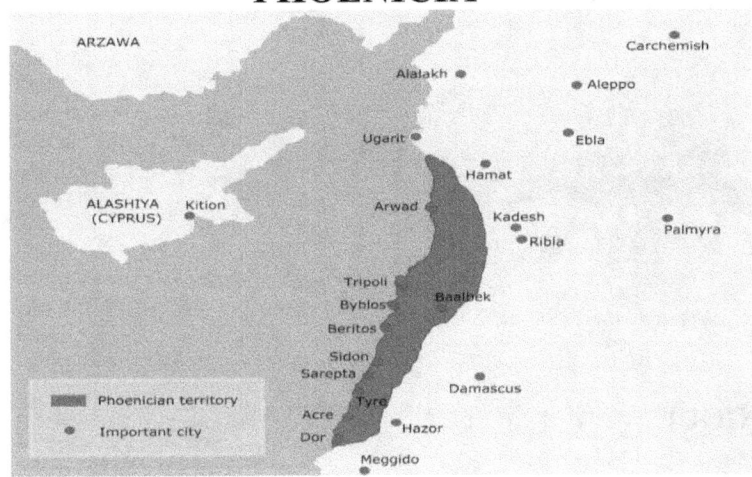

LEBANON

THE ARAB WORLD

PREFACE

WHAT MAKES THIS TEXTBOOK UNIQUE?

This book does away with the myth, widely believed by students, that Modern Standard Arabic (MSA), which is primarily written Arabic, enables you to speak with ordinary people in the street. This course does the pioneering work of presenting, contextually, a comprehensive grammar of Lebanese Arabic. Lebanese is the dialect that belongs to the Levantine family of dialects, spoken also in Jordan, Palestine and Syria. The Arabic used in everyday oral communication between the Lebanese enables you to communicate effectively throughout the MiddleeEast.

WHY LEARN SPOKEN ARABIC (A DIALECT)?

Unlike Standard English, as previously mentioned, Modern Standard Arabic is not spoken in everyday conversation. Standard Arabic is confined to the media, literature, letter writing, and formal speech making and interviews. People use dialect to speak with each other. Using Standard Arabic in shops, on the bus or to ask for directions is likely to be met with a smile. What's more, the average native speaker would be reluctant to respond in MSA. Having had no practice, though they may be able to somehow manage the task, they will find it awkwardly artificial. It is like using Shakespearean English to buy a loaf of bread. It is like saying: 'How art thou?' instead of 'How are you?'

Any MiddleeEastern dialect would help you communicate from Iraq in the east, to Yemen in the south, and to Egypt in the west. However, Tunisia, Libya, Algeria and Morocco have their own family of dialects. These North-African dialects of Arabic would need exposure to and some getting used to by a MiddleeEasterner before communication may start to flow.

Egyptian, Lebanese and Syrian are the most widely understood dialects in the Arab world. This is thanks to television and cinema. Their own prolifically produced popular films and/or soaps, along with those dubbed from other languages into Lebanese and Syrian and widely distributed, have further enhanced these three dialects' exposure. Lebanese and Egyptian songs are also the most extensively listened to.

FOCUS OF THIS BOOK

WHO MAY USE THIS BOOK
This book has been designed to be used by:
- teachers and students in a **classroom** setting.
- **independent learners,** who will be equally successful if they work through its easy-to-follow instruction and exercises.

BALANCE
In this book there is a balance of listening, speaking, reading, and writing activities, along with dialogues and written texts.

AIM
To understand spoken Arabic and speak in everyday situations, thanks to the Lebanese dialect.
> **NOTE** As stated earlier, the Lebanese dialect belongs to the Levantine family of Arabic dialects used also in Syria, Palestine and Jordan. Although their use diminishes with distance from these countries, the Lebanese dialect will be largely familiar and remain helpful throughout the rest of the Arab world, thanks to film, television, soap operas, theatre, and prolific song distribution and broadcasts.

OBJECTIVES
Students will be able to understand and communicate in Lebanese / Levantine / spoken Arabic, using typical language for everyday situations.

EACH UNIT CONTAINS THE FOLLOWING SECTIONS:
DIALOGUE: To model spoken expression and correct intonation in contextual settings.
CULTURE: To provide information regarding the etiquete, way of life, geography and history of the Lebanese in the framework of their presence between the rest of the Arab world and Europe. The cultural notes are reflected in and throw light on the behaviors and language use of the Lebanese.
VOCABULARY: To enrich the spoken word/expression bank.
GRAMMAR: To learn the rules and structures that govern oral speech and, in particular, the Lebanese dialect.
COMPREHEND & COMMUNICATE: To boost oral understanding and confidence while speaking in simulated everyday situations.

- All sections contain **exercises** to provide practice that helps build on the old and master newly acquired language.
- The **listening** exercises expose students' ears to the dialect. They give students the opportunity to model their **pronunciation** on typical, contextually used language.
- Key topic-related **conversational questions and answers** are shaded for easy spotting.

FLUENCY
As with any language, practice makes perfect. Thus, language acquisition is incremental. By the end of this book, a student's level should range between the ability to get by and fluency. Progress will depend on how much time and effort are devoted to mastering the content of the units.

TABLE OF CONTENTS

UNIT	Page	TYPICAL QUESTION	CULTURE	VOCABULARY	GRAMMAR
1	1	Hello! What's your name?	Names	Greetings	. Pronouns . Possessive suffixes . Consonant cluster 'i'
2	4	How are you?	Personal closeness	Feeling	. Personal suffixes . Adjectives mfp . Two long syllables in succession
3	7	Where are you from?	Lebanon's geography	Nationality	. Nationality mfp . Feminine ending a/e
4	10	What's your address and phone number?	. Courting . Finding an address	. Address . Phone number	. Negating nouns and adjectives
5	14	What do you do for a living?	Working hours	Occupation	. Plural: human nouns . Present tense . Vowel drop before suffix
6	18	Do you come from a large family?	Family relations	Family	. Number + noun
7	22	What would you like to drink?	Eating etiquette	Cafe	. Plural: non-human nouns . Article: a/the . Present . Negation . Dropping 'b' . Imperative + its negation . Polite requests
8	27	What did you do last week/end?	Lebanese pastimes	Every-day activities	. Past tense . ee (non-guttural) / aa (guttural)
9	31	What are you doing next week/end?	Healthcare	Describing people and things	. Plural of adjectives . Future . All tense negation of adjectives
10	35	What's the time/date?	. Pace of life . Hijri year	. Time . Date . Days . Months . Seasons	. Present continuous tense

UNIT	Page	TYPICAL QUESTION	CULTURE	VOCABULARY	GRAMMAR
11	40	Where is the museum?	Transport	. Places . Transport . Directions	. Past + future continuous tenses . Verb object suffixes after consonant and vowel
12	45	Can I book a room for two?	Hotel accommodation	Hotel	. Comparison . 2nd object pronoun
13	49	What would you like to eat?	Meeza	Restaurant	. Feminine pronounced as 'it' . ee > ay . Double middle consonant . 'Saying' verbs
14	54	How much are the shoes?	Shopping	. Shopping . Colours . Ordinal numbers	. To/for before personal suffix . Ordinal numbers
15	59	What are your hobbies?	Typical Lebanese hobbies	Hobbies	. Participle . Passive . Preposition/adverb + ma
16	64	. Where would you like to travel to? . What's the weather like?	Tourism	. Tourism . Weather	. Conditional . Root derivations

68   Answers & transcripts

80   Appendix 1   Question words, prepositions, conjunctions
81   Appendix 2   Verb conjugation
83   Appendix 3   Verb-tense comparison

84   Glossary: Lebanese   >   English
92   Glossary: English   >   Lebanese

100   Index

PRONUNCIATION KEY

This pronunciation key **must be mastered before the student starts the units**, to ensure that their pronunciation will be accurate and that what they learn and say will be well understood.

VOWELS

Arabic has two types of vowels: long and short. In this book, long vowels are hyphenated to distinguish them from short vowels.

 Listen and repeat the following, noting the sound difference between short and long vowels:

short	long (with hyphen)	as in the following sounds (in bold type) in English words:	
a		at / hut	
	aa		ant / art
e		bet	
	ee		bear
i		him	
	ii		heat
o		hot	
	oo		hall
u		foot	
	uu		a long oo in fooot

GUTTURAL CONSONANTS

CAPITALISED LETTERS

Some ordinary consonants have also guttural equivalents. In this book, the guttural equivalents of ordinary consonants are capitalised for clear distinction. As in English, ordinary letters are uttered from the front part of the mouth. The guttural equivalents, however, come from the back of the mouth or the throat.

 Listen and repeat: the ordinary consonant, its guttural equivalent, and its example word:

Ordinary letter	Guttural equivalent	Example
s	S	Saff [class]
d	D	Daww [light]
t	T	Taawle [table]
k	Q	Qur2aan [Quran]
z	Z	Zarf [envelope]

TWINNED CONSONANTS (ending in 'h'):

 Listen and repeat the following guttural consonants. They have no ordinary letter equivalents:

Letter combination	How the sound is made	Example
gh	as sound made when gargling	ghayme [cloud]
kh	as in Lo**ch** Ness Monster	khaatim [ring]

NUMBERS

Numbers represent other letter sounds that do not exist in the English alphabet (see table below). These numbers have been chosen, as they look somewhat like the Arabic letter in reverse.

 Listen and repeat the following guttural letters, represented by a number, and their example words:

Number	How the sound is made	Example
2	as sound made when starting the English vowels (a, e, i, o)	2ism [name]
7	breathy, as when you have lost your voice	7ilm [dream]
3	as sound made when you dry retch	3ilm [education]

Note: j is pronounced without the d sound ~~d~~j, as in **pleasure** not as in George.

UNIT 1

UNIT 1
What's your name?

DIALOGUE

1 greetings | **name** 2 feeling 3 nationality 4 address | phone no. 5 occupation 6 family 7 cafe 8 past activities 9 future activities
10 time | date | activity now 11 places | transport | directions 12 hotel 13 restaurant 14 shopping 15 pastimes | taste 16 tourism | weather

 (Refer to the **pronunciation key** on the previous page to read the following dialogue.)

NOTE 1.1 HOW TO READ:
1 Arabic is a phonetic language. All **consonants must be pronounced**, including those at the **end of a syllable/word**.
2 Count the **number of vowels** of a word before reading it, as they should match the **number of syllables** you read.
3 Every **syllable must start with a consonant** whether at the beginning, middle, or end of a word.
4 Only a **consonant that is followed by/has a vowel** starts a syllable. A consonant that is not followed by a vowel ends a syllable.
5 **Pause between syllables** until the word becomes familiar enough to be accurately pronounced without the pause.
(This will also apply to the Arabic script when we get to it)

Samiir & Layla

   Samir & Layla

Samir	mar7aba[hello]. 2ana[I] 2isme[name] samiir, w[and] 7aDirtik[you], shu[what] 2ismik?
Layla	2ahlan [pleased to meet you] samiir. 2ana 2isme layla.
Samir	tsharrafna[pleased to meet you], layla.
Layla	bkhaaTrak[bye], samiir.
Samir	ma3 i ssaleeme[bye], layla.

 1.1
1 shu[what's] 2ismo[his name]?
2 shu 2isma[her name]? (ANSWERS page 68)

CULTURE

NAMES

Arab names can be:
Muslim:	m7ammad	3ale [Ali]	khadiije	faaTme
Christian	7anna [John]	buTrus [Peter]	marii [Mary]	2elizabeet
Arabic (shared by both)	7abiib	samiir	layla	wafaa2

UNIT 1

VOCABULARY

GREETINGS

Hello	mar7aba > 2ahlan (response)
Good morning	Sabaa7 i lkheer
Good evening	masa lkheer

GOODBYE

	Masculine	Feminine	Plural
Goodbye (Person leaving)	bkhaaTr**ak**	bkhaaTr**ik**	bkhaaTir**kun**
Goodbye (Person staying)	ma3 i ssaleeme			

1.2 Respond: eg **masa lkheer** > **2ahlan / masa lkheer**

1 Sabaa7 i lkheer   2 mar7aba   3 masa lkheer   4 bkhaaTirkun   5 bkhaaTrak   6 bkhaaTrik

1.3 Find five vocabulary words/phrases in the find-a-word:

z	x	t	s	h	a	r	r	a	f	n	a
f	v	c	m	a	s	a	l	k	h	ee	r
Q	y	w	2	a	h	l	a	n	h	r	h
f	x	g	7	a	D	i	r	t	a	k	j
S	a	b	aa	7	i	l	k	h	ee	r	k

GRAMMAR language rules

Person	PRONOUNS replace noun		POSSESSIVE SUFFIXES endings		
1st	I (am)	2ana	my name (is)	2ism	**e**
	we (are)	ni7**na**	our name (is)	2isim	**na**
2nd	you (are) masculine	2int**a**	your name (is) m	2ism	**ak**
	you (are) feminine	2int**e**	your name (is) f	2ism	**ik**
	you (are) plural	2int**o**	your name (is) p	2isim	**kun**
3rd	he (is)	huw**we**	his name (is)	2ism	**o**
	she (is)	hi**yye**	her name (is)	2ism	**a**
	they (are)	hi**nne**	their name (is)	2ism	**un**

RULE 1.4 Where there are **three or more consonants in a row**, count two consonants back from the end of that cluster and insert the sound **i** to facilitate pronunciation (see 2isimna^our / 2isimkun^your pl).

Exception: A double consonant initiating a cluster cannot be split
  eg marrteen^twice. 2 syllables: marr teen and not ma~~ri~~rteen

1.4 Referring to the above rule, rewrite the following words, inserting the **i** sound where needed:
  1 2isma   2 2ismkun   3 2ismun   4 2ismna   5 2ismik

1.5 What's the pronoun? eg 2ismo > **huwwe**
  1 2ismak   2 2isimna   3 2ismik   4 2isme   5 2ismun   6 2isimkun

1.6 What's the possessive ending? eg 2inta > **shu 2ism**ak**?**
  1 hiyye   2 hinne   3 2inta   4 2into   5 huwwe   6 2ana

UNIT 1

 1.7 What's the person's name? eg shu 2ismak? samiir > 2isme samiir.
    1 shu 2ismik? layla   3 shu 2ismo? 7abiib   5 shu 2ismun? 3ale w faaTme
    2 shu 2isma? 2elizabeet   4 shu 2isimkun? tom w saam   6 shu 2ismak? buTrus

*Respectful	Masculine	Feminine	Plural
You	7aDirtak	7aDirtik	7aDritkun

Pleased to meet you	2ahlan / tsharrafna

*The **respectful you** is used when you meet someone for the first time or they are of high standing in the community.

 1.8 Use 'and you' eg you^m|friend   > w^{and} **2inta,**   shu 2ismak?
                     you^m|stranger   > w **7aDirtak,**   shu 2ismak?
  1 you^f|friend   2 you^p|classmates   3 you^m|toddler   4 you^f|president   5 you^m|new student   6 you^p|children

 1.9 Respond:
1 mar7aba.   2 2isme samiir, w 7aDirtik?   3 2ana 2isme saam.   4 bkhaaTrak, saam.   5 bkhaaTirkun

COMPREHEND & COMMUNICATE

1.10 Listen and, based on your understanding of the dialogue, put an **X** in the appropriate column:

	a	b	c	d	e	f	g
Sa7^{true}							
ghalaT^{false}							

 1.11 What variations can you give for what is in bold type?
      eg 'mar7aba' can be replaced with 'Sabaa7 i lkheer' etc...

su2aal^{question}	jaweeb^{answer}
mar7aba. 2isme layla. w **2inta,** shu 2ismak?	**tsharrafna**, layla, (2ana) 2isme samiir. bkhaaT**rik**.

(What is in brackets is optional)

1.12 Exchange names with a couple of other (real or imaginary) individuals.

1.13 Prepare a **sketch**: Three or more people meet for the first time and exchange greetings, names, and goodbyes.

UNIT 2
How are you?

DIALOGUE

1 greetings | name 2 **feeling** 3 nationality 4 address | phone no. 5 occupation 6 family 7 cafe 8 past activities 9 future activities 10 time | date | activity now 11 places | transport | directions 12 hotel 13 restaurant 14 shopping 15 pastimes | taste 16 tourism | weather

      samiir w layla

1 Samir   mar7aba, layla. kiifik^{how are you} lyoom^{today}?

2 Layla   mnii7a^{well}, shukran^{thank you}, w 2inta?

3 Samir   2ana mish^{not} ktiir^{very} mnii7. Saakhin^{sick} shwayy^{a little}.

4 Layla   saleemtak^{I wish you a speedy recovery}, samiir.

5 Samir   shukran, layla. bkhaaTrik. raayi7^{I'm going} neem^{sleep}.

6 Layla   ma3 i ssaleeme, samiir.

1 Hi, Layla. How are you today?

2 I'm well, thank you, and you?

3 I'm not very well. I'm a little sick.

4 I wish you a speedy recovery, Samir.

5 Thank you, Layla. Bye, I'm off to sleep.

6 Bye, Samir.

 2.1

    1 kiifa layla lyoom?

    2 kiifo samiir?

CULTURE

PERSONAL CLOSENESS

'How are you?' in the Middle East is often not a token part of a greeting. Given that the culture is based on close community and family ties, the question is likely to be one that encourages and receives a genuine response. Rather than just an 'I'm fine, thank you,' the answer may be one of a spectrum of states the person could be feeling at the time. The person may not shy away from giving details if they are sick, or explaining circumstances. This may lead to news giving and gossip or serve as a lubricant for a chit-chat. That is often followed by an invitation to their house for a coffee.

Don't be surprised if frequent terms of warm endearment are exchanged, '7abiibe' *My dear/love*, '2alla yishfiik' *May God heal you*, 'ti2birne' *May you bury me* (which means: *May you outlive me*), etc....

GRAMMAR

PERSONAL SUFFIXES

 2.2 Follow the 2ism + **possessive suffixes'** model (see 1.4) to complete the pronominal suffixes for **kiif**:

How am I?	kiif	ne?
How are we?	kiif	na?
How are you?ᵐ	kiif	...
How are you?ᶠ	kiif	...
How are you?ᵖ	kiif	...
How is he?	kiif	...
How is she?	kiif	...
How are they?	kiif	...

2.3 Ask: eg 2inta > **kiifak?**

1 2into 2 hiyye 3 huwwe 4 ni7na 5 hinne 6 2inte

UNIT 2

VOCABULARY

ADJECTIVES: MASCULINE, FEMININE & PLURAL ENDINGS

2.4 Fill in the blanks in the table:

RULE 2.4
- When the adjective ends with a **guttural** letter, you form the feminine by adding **a** eg mnii7a
- When the adjective ends with a **non-guttural** letter, you form the feminine by adding **e** eg ti3beene
- The common plural ending is **iin** eg ti3ben**iin**, Sakhn**iin**

FEELING	Adverb	Masculine	Feminine	Plural
well		mnii7[good]	mnii7a	mnee7
very well	ktiir	...	...	...
not well	mish	...	...	...
a little tired	shwayy	ti3been	ti3beene	*ti3beniin
a little sick	...	Saakhin	Saakhn...	*Sakhn...
so so	heek heek			

*NOTE 2.4 Where there are **two long vowels in a row**, you can shorten the first, eg ti3been[m], ti3beene[f], but ti3beniin[p]

2.5 Answer: eg kiifak? > **ktiir mnii7**

1 kiifa? 2 kiifak? 3 kiifun? 4 kiifkun? 5 kiifik?

COMPREHEND & COMMUNICATE

2.6 Listen and, based on your understanding of the dialogue, put an **X** in the appropriate column:

	a	b	c	d	e	f	g
Sa7[true]							
ghalaT[false]							

2.7 What variations can you give for what is in bold type?

su2aal[question]	jaweeb[answer]
kiifak?	**ktiir mnii7**, shukran[thank you], w 2inta?

2.8 Ask and exchange how you feel with a couple of other (real or imaginary) individuals.

2.9 Prepare a **sketch**: Three people meet. One person is new; the other two are friends. Include greetings, how everyone is feeling, and goodbyes.

UNIT 3
Where are you from?

DIALOGUE

1 greetings | name 2 feeling **3 nationality** 4 address | phone no. 5 occupation 6 family 7 cafe 8 past activities 9 future activities
10 time | date | activity now 11 places | transport | directions 12 hotel 13 restaurant 14 shopping 15 pastimes | taste 16 tourism | weather

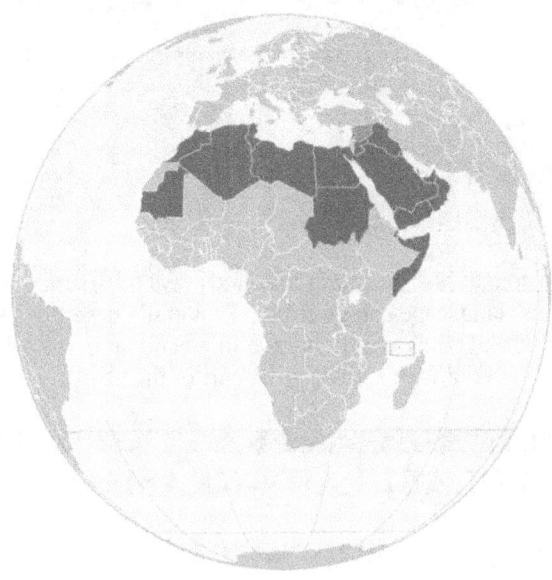

 samiir w layla w tom

1 Samir	mar7aba. kiifkun lyoom?	
2 Layla	2ana mnii7a, w 2into?	
3 Tom	2ana ti3been w Saakhin shwayy. w 2inta, samiir?	
4 Samir	kint[was] Saakhin, bas[but] halla2[now] Sirt[become] 2a7san[better], shukran.	
5 Layla	2inta min[from] ween[where], tom?	
6 Tom	2ana 2ostraale[Australian] w seekin[live] bi[in] sidni bi 2ostraalya, w 2into?	
7 Layla	baladak[country] ktiir b3iid![far] ni7na libneniyye[Lebanese] min hoon[here].	
8 Tom	niyyeelkun[lucky you], baladkun ktiir 7ilo[beautiful].	
9 Layla	shukran, tom, 2inta ktiir laTiif[kind]. w halla2 2ana leezim[must] ruu7[go]. 3inde[have] maw3id [appointment]. bkhaaTirkun.	
10 T&S	ma3 i ssaleeme, layla.	

1 Hi. How are you today?
2 I'm well, and you?
3 I'm tired and a little sick, and you, Samir?
4 I was sick, I'm feeling better now, thank you.
5 Where are you from, Tom?
6 I'm Australian and I live in Sydney, Australia, and you?
7 Your country is very far! We're Lebanese from here.
8 I wish I were so lucky! Your country is very beautiful.
9 Thank you, Tom, you're very kind. And now I must go. I have an appointment. Bye.
10 Bye, Layla.

 3.1
1 min ween samiir w layla?
2 tom min ween?

UNIT 3

CULTURE
ARAB WORLD GEOGRAPHY

The Arab world spans twenty-two countries. Their traditions and ways of life may be as varied as the terrain and climate they live in. The inhabitants' landscape can go from a Bedouin's desert oasis to a thriving modern city such as Beirut. Their activities may vary from being part of a travelling caravan in the arid desert to skiing on the chic slopes of the Lebanese mountains, covered with snow a great part of the year.

VOCABULARY-GRAMMAR

NATIONALITIES

NOTE 3.2a
- The masculine of nationalities ends in   **e**   eg huwwe   2ostraa**e**
- The feminine of nationalities ends in   **iyye**   eg hiyye   2ostral**iyye**
- There are **two plural categories** for nationalities (These become familiar through general reading):
  - one, like the feminine, ends in   **iyye**, eg hinne 2ostral**iyye**   (see Category 1 below)
  - the other is like the masculine but without   **e**   eg hinne 2amerkeen   (see Category 2 below)

3.2 Noting the two plural categories, complete the following table:

NOTE 3.2b A long vowel followed by a double consonnant is shortened. eg 2ostraale, but 2ostraliyye

balad^{country}	mdiine^{city} / 3aaSme^{capital}	jinsiyye^{nationality} / 2aSl^{origins}		
		Masculine	Feminine	Plural
		Category 1		
2ostraalya	kanbeera	2ostraale	2ostraliyye	
libneen	bayruut	libneen ...	...	
hollanda	2amsterdam	holland ...	...	
2irlanda	dablin	2irland ...	...	
		Category 2		
2ameerka	washinton	2amerkeene	2amerkeniyye	2amerkeen
2almaanya	berliin	2almaan ...	2alman ...	2almaan
*lyabaan	tookyo	yabaan ...	yaban ...	...
*SSiin	bejiin	Siin ...	Sin ...	...

*When a word starts with **l** or a **double consonant**, that's the equivalent of 'the' in English. Arabic says *The Japan, The China*. English says *The Philippines*.

3.3 Match the country with the nationality:
     1 2ingliteerra   2 skotlanda   3 2iTaalya   4 2espaanya   5 fransa   6 rusiyya
     a skotlande^{C1}   b frinseewe^{C1}   c spanyoole^{C2}   d ruuse^{C2}   e tilyeene^{C2}   f 2ingliize^{C2}

UNIT 3

3.4 Give the feminine and plural of the nationality eg skotlande^m > skotlandiyye^f > skotlandiyye^p
 1 braziile^C1 2 frinseewe^C1 3 spanyoole^C2 4 ruuse^C2 5 tilyeene^C2 6 2ingliize^C2

3.5 Ask: eg you^m > **2inta** min ween?^(where are you from?)
 1 they 2 you^f 3 he 4 you^m 5 you^p 6 we

3.6 Answer: eg 2inta min ween? | SSiin > 2ana **Siine**
 1 2inta min ween? | lyabaan   2 2into min ween | 2almaanya   3 ni7na min ween? | libneen
 4 huwwe min ween | 2irlanda   5 hinne min ween | 2ostraalya   6 2inte min ween | 2ameerka

3.7 Ask: eg you^m > bas^but **2aSlak**^(e\na....) min ween?^(where are you originally from?)
 1 they 2 you^f 3 he 4 you^m 5 you^p 6 we

3.8 Answer: eg > bas^but 2aSlak min ween? | taylanda^C1 2aSle **taylande**.
1 bas 2aSlak min ween? | lmeksiik^C1   3 bas 2aSilkun min ween? ^Iraql3iraa2^C1 5 bas 2aSlo min ween | ^(see 3.3b)fransa^C1
2 bas 2aSlik min ween? | nyuzilanda^C1   4 bas 2aSla min ween? | swiisra^C1   6 bas 2aSlun min ween? | ^Greece lyuneen^C2

FEMININE NOUNS

NOTE 3.9 In general, Arabic nouns that end in **e/a** (a follows a guttural letter) are feminine. Those that don't are masculine.

3.9 Circle feminine words and put a square around masculine words:
 1 hollanda 2 libneen 3 siyyaara^car 4 2ism 5 balad 6 mdiine

COMPREHEND & COMMUNICATE

3.10 Listen and, based on your understanding of the dialogue, put an **X** in the appropriate column:

	a	b	c	d	e	f	g
Sa7							
ghalaT							

3.11 What variations can you give for what is in bold type?

su2aal\2as2ile^(question\s)	jaweeb\2ajwibe^(answer\s)
2inta min ween?	2ana **2ostraale** / min **2ostraalya**
bas **2aSlak** min ween?	**2aSle 2ingliize** / min **2ingliteerra**

3.12 Exchange nationalities and origins with a couple of other (real or imaginary) individuals.

3.13 Prepare a **sketch**: A few people meet, greet, exchange names, feelings, nationalities and goodbyes.

UNIT 4
Where do you live?

10

DIALOGUE

1 greetings | name 2 feeling 3 nationality 4 address | phone no. 5 occupation 6 family 7 cafe 8 past activities 9 future activities 10 time | date | activity now 11 places | transport | directions 12 hotel 13 restaurant 14 shopping 15 pastimes | taste 16 tourism | weather

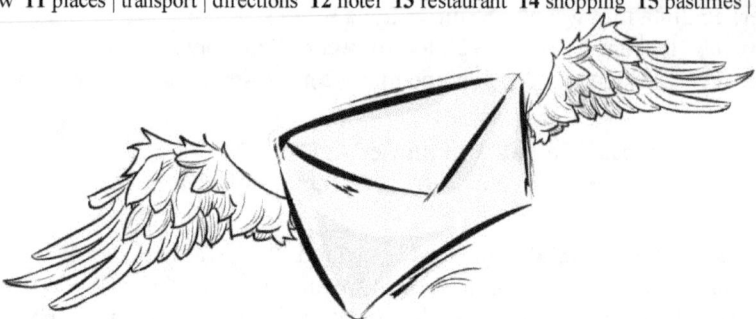

samiir w layla w tom
1 S Sabaa7 lkheer, layla. nshalla[I hope] mnii7a?
2 L 2ana heek heek lyoom. w 2into kiifkun?
3 S 2ana Sirt ktiir mnii7, l7amdilla[praise be to God].
4 T w 2ana kameen[also] Sirt mnii7, shukran.
5 S tom, shu 3inweenak[address] bi sidni? barke[maybe] breeslak[I'll correspond with you] huniik[there].
6 T seekin bi raandwik, sheeri3[street] king, ra2m[number] khamse[five].
7 S w shu numrit[number of] talifoonak[phone] huniik?
8 T ra2m talifoone 0415 736 298
9 S w 2inte, layla, shu 3inweenik w ra2m talifoonik?
10 L *ya[oh] samiir, 2ana ma[don't] ba3Te[give] 3inweene w numrit talifoone bi[at] hayde[this] ssir3a[speed].
11 S ma3leesh[never mind] barke lmarra[time] ljeey[next].
12 L bkhaaTirkun.
13 S &T   ma3 i ssaleeme, layla.

*ya [oh] is used before a name to show the increased attention you are paying[oh] the person, or to call[Hey!] for their attention.

1 Good morning, Layla. I hope you're well.
2 I'm feeling sooso today, and you?
3 I'm now feeling very well, God be praised.
4 And also I am feeling good now, thank you.
5 Tom, what's your address in Sydney? maybe I'll correspond with you there.
6 I live at 5 King Street, Randwick (Note the reverse order in Arabic).
7 And what's your phone number there?
8 My phone number is 0415 736 298.
9 And you, Layla, what's your address and phone number?
10 Samir, I don't give my address and phone number so quickly.
11 Never mind, maybe next time.
12 Bye.
13 Bye, Layla.

 4.1

1 kiifa layla lyoom?
2 kiifo samiir?
3 min ween tom?
4 shu 3inweeno?
5 shu ra2m talifoono? (See numbers on next page)
6 shu ma bta3Te layla la[to] samiir?

UNIT 4

CULTURE

COURTING AND ADDRESS FINDING

Despite Lebanon being relatively liberal by comparison to other Arab countries, tradition, community, and family have a strong influence on the decisions individuals make, especially in villages.

A girl is advised to act hard to get and have the man make an effort before showing her true feelings for him.

A young man feels under pressure to meet the family before taking a girl out. It is not uncommon for parents to demand that the girl be chaperoned by another family member when she goes out on a date. A suitor is encouraged to declare his marriage intent and get engaged if he wants to continue to see her with the family's blessing.

By and large, young people tend to live at home until they get married.

An address is more likely to be known or found by the mention of a local landmark or a well-known person associated with the area.

VOCABULARY

NUMBERS l2ar2aam

4.2 With the rule and reminder below in mind complete the following number patterns:

٠	0	Sifir	١٠	10	3ashra						
١	1	waa7ad	١١	11	7da3sh				٢١	21	wa7daw 3ishriin
٢	2	tneen	١٢	12	tna3sh	٢٠	20	3ishriin	٢٢	22	tneenaw ...
٣	3	tleete	١٣	13	tletta3sh	٣٠	30	tletiin	٣٣	33	tleet ...
٤	4	2arb3a	١٤	14	2arba3ta3sh	٤٠	40	2arb3...	٤٤	44	2arb3 ...
٥	5	khamse	١٥	15	khamis ...	٥٠	50	khams...	٥٥	55	...
٦	6	sitte	١٦	16	sit ...	٦٠	60	sitt ...	٦٦	66	...
٧	7	sab3a	١٧	17	saba3 ...	٧٠	70	sab3 ...	٧٧	77	...
٨	8	tmeene	١٨	18	tmen ...	٨٠	80	tmen ...	٨٨	88	...
٩	9	tis3a	١٩	19	tisa3 ...	٩٠	90	tis3 ...	٩٩	99	...

RULE 4.2 Apart from for 1 and 2, when you add a syllable/word, remove the short vowel of the preceding syllable
eg when you add to tleete, **ta3sh**, remove the **e** of te. You end up with tlee**tta3sh**.
REMINDER If you are left with three or more consonants in a row, count two from the end and insert **i** or
a if what was removed was **a** eg 2arb3a becomes 2arb**a**3ta3sh and not 2arb**i**3ta3sh.

 4.3 Ask: eg 5 + 3 > 2addeesh$^{how\ much}$ **khamse w tleete?**(Choose: w^{plus} naa2iS^{minus} 3a$^{divided\ by}$ bi^{times})
a 7 – 4   b 8 % 2   c 90 % 3   d 5 x 8   e 13 + 28   f 78 – 43

 4.4 Do the sums: eg khamse w tleete bya3imlo^{make} **tmeene**.
1 tmeene naa2iS 2arb3a ...   3 2arb3iin 3a tneen ...   5 khamsta3sh w 3ashra ...
2 tis3a 3a tleete ...   4 tneen bi tleete ...   6 2arb3iin naa2iS khamse ...

 4.5 Complete the table:

١٠٠	100	miyye	٢٠٠	200	miteen	٣٠٠	300	tleet miyye
١٠١	101	miyye w waa7ad	٢٠٤	204	miteen w 2arb3a	٤٠٧	407	2arba3 miyye w sab3a
...	102	...	...	205	miteen w ...	...	508	...
...	103	...	...	206	...	...	609	...

UNIT 4

4.6 Start from the number and continue up another two: eg 100 > miyye, miyye w waa7ad, miyye w tneen.
  a 107   b 233   c 310   d 409   e 580   f 900

4.7 Complete the table:

١٠٠٠	1000	2alf	٢٠٠٠	2000	2alfeen	1m	malyoon	1b	milyaar
١٠٠١	1001	2alf w waa7ad	٢٠٠٣	2003	...	1m5	malyoon w khamse	1b7	...
...	1002	...	...	2004	...	1m6	...	1b8	...
...	1003	...	...	2005	...	1m7	...	1b9	...

4.8 Ask & answer: eg mikel2angelo | 1564 > 2imtiin[when] meet[died] mikel2angelo?
bi[in] sint[year] l2alf w khams miyye w 2arb3aw sittiin.

1 nelson mandella | 2013 3 ma7atma ghaandi | 1948 5 nnabe[prophet] m7ammad | 632
2 hitler | 1945 4 bethoven | 1827 6 nappolyoon | 1821

GRAMMAR

POSSESSIVE SUFFIXES with feminine nouns

4.9 Complete the following table (see 2ism endings in 1.4):
NOTE 4.9 Before you can add a suffix to a feminine word, replace its **a/e** with **t**
  eg siyyaara > siyyaarte[my car]. dayne[ear] > dayintak[your ear].
REMEMBER The consonant cluster rule (how **i** may shift), and the preceding vowel dropped when a suffix is added[see 4.2]

	Masculine			Feminine						*Exception: If
				siyyaara		[number]numra		dayne		cluster 'i' was used
2ana	3inwen|e		sheer3|e	siyyaar|te		numir|te		dayin|te		for ni7na, for **hiyye**
ni7na		na	sheeri3|na	siyyaarit|na		numrit|na		daynit|na	and **hinne** 'i' must
2inta	...	...	...	...	...	...	...	...	...	be placed before
2inte	...	...	...	...	...	...	...	...	...	the last consonant
2into	...	...	...	...	...	...	...	...	...	and stressed, even
huwwe	...	...	...	...	...	...	...	...	...	though there's no
hiyye		...	*sheeri3	...	*siyyaarit	...	*numrit	...	...	...	consonant cluster
hinne		...	*sheeri3	...	*siyyaarit	...	*numrit	...	...	...	there.

4.10 Say whose it is: eg dayne | huwwe > hayde[this is] **dayinto** (Choose: hayda[m] / hayde[f])
1 2alam[pen]|2inta 2 kteeb[book]|2inte 3 shanta[bag]|huwwe 4 siyyaara|2ana 5 kalb[dog]|ni7na 6 zahra[flower]|hinne

4.11 Read the rule below before asking the questions: eg dayne > hayde **daynit** miin?

RULE 4.11 Even if no suffix is added, the e/a ending of a feminine noun turns into and is pronounced as **it** in spoken if the word **'of'** can be used in English. eg siyyaara, but hayde siyyar**it** miin? *The car of whom = whose car is this?*
  1 kteeb 2 siyyaara 3 zahra 4 kalb 5 2alam 6 shanta

NEGATING NOUNS & ADJECTIVES

RULE 4.12 To negate nouns and adjectives use **mish**[not] eg 2ana mish ti3been. hayde mish siyyaarte.

4.12 Answer: eg 2inta ti3been? No > **la2**, 2ana **mish** ti3been.
(Choose from: 2e[yes(familiar)]/na3am[yes(formal)]/la2[no])

1 7aDirtik yabaniyye? Yes 3 hiyye ti3beene? Yes 5 7aDirtak 2ingliize? Yes
2 hayda kteebak? No 4 huwwe Saakhin? No 6 hayde shantitun? No

UNIT 4

COMPREHEND & COMMUNICATE

4.13 Listen and, based on your understanding of the dialogue, put an **X** in the appropriate column:

	a	b	c	d	e	f	g	h
Sa7								
ghalaT								

4.14 ghayyro[change] lkalimeet[words] yalle[which] |b khaTT ghaami2|[bold type]:

su2aal\2as2ile[question\s]	jaweeb\2ajwibe[answer\s]
ween *seek**in**?	seekin bi[in] raandwick
shu 3inweenak?	seekin bi **raandwick**, sheeri3 **king**, ra2m **khamse**
shu **numr**it talifoon**ak**?/shu nu**mir**tak?	**ra2m** talifoone 0415873426

*seekin[live] behaves like an adjective eg seekin[e\iin], just like ti3been[e\iin]

4.15 tbeedalo[exchange] addresses and phone numbers with a couple of other (real or imaginary) individuals.

4.16 Prepare a **sketch** with a:

   beginning (Greetings/scene setting)

   middle (A problem arises)   eg a person accidently gives the wrong address and phone number.

   end (The problem is resolved)   eg a third person corrects the details.

4.17 t7addaso[Converse] (tzakkaro[recall] l2as2ile[questions] w l2ajwibe[answers]):

   1 greetings | name   **2** feeling   **3** nationality   **4 address**   **1** goodbye

UNIT 5

UNIT 5
What do you do for a living?

DIALOGUE

1 greetings | name 2 feeling 3 nationality 4 address | phone no. 5 occupation 6 family 7 cafe 8 past activities 9 future activities 10 time | date | activity now 11 places | transport | directions 12 hotel 13 restaurant 14 shopping 15 pastimes | taste 16 tourism | weather

     samiir w layla
1 S masa lkheer, layla. kiifik?
2 L |meeshe l7aal|[fine], shukran, w 2inta?
3 S 2ana kameen[also] mnii7 lyoom, shukran.
4 L 2inta shu btishtighil[do you work as], ya samiir?
5 S 2ana m3allim[teacher] bi[in] madrase[school] bi bayruut. w 2inte shu btishtighle?
6 L 2ana Tibbaakha[cook].
7 S bas ween[where] btishtighle ka[as] Tibbaakha?
8 L bishtighil[I work] bi maTbakh[kitchen].
9 S 2aSde[I mean] shu 3inween shighlik?
10 L bi3tizir[sorry], samiir, bas 2ana ma ba3Te 3inween lbeet[house] 2aw[or] shshighil bi hayde ssir3a.
11 S Tayyib[ok], ma3leesh. barke lmarra ljeey.
12 L bkhaTrak, samiir.
13 S ma3 i ssaleeme, layla. sallme[give my regards].

1 Good evening, Layla. How are you?
2 Fine, thanks, and you?
3 Also I am well today, thank you.
4 What do you do for a living, Samir?
5 I'm a teacher in a school in Beirut. And you, what do you do?
6 I'm a cook.
7 But where do you work as a cook?
8 I work in a kitchen.
9 I mean, what's the address of your work?
10 Sorry, Samir, but I don't give my home or work address so quickly.
11 Ok. Never mind. Maybe next time.
12 Bye, Samir.
13 Bye, Layla. Give my regards.

 5.1

    1 kiifo samir lyoom?
    2 shu byishtighil samiir?
    3 ween byishtighil samiir?
    4 shu btishtighil layla?
    5 ween btishtighil layla?
    6 bta3Te layla samiir 3inween bayta[house] w shighla[work]? (2e 2aw[or] la2?)

CULTURE

WORKING HOURS

In Lebanon it is not uncommon for shops to open and for workers to start work mid-morning. People go out or stay up socialising late with family and friends. Lunch break can be up to two or three hours long. That is enough time to eat and have an afternoon nap; much appreciated in the warmer parts of the year. One then restarts mid-afternoon and finishes late evening. Remember, it is a culture that has personal relations and socialising at its heart.

VOCABULARY

OCCUPATIONS

5.2 Follow the given models to complete the table, with the note and reminder below in mind:

NOTE 5.2 a. For **nouns** referring to **humans**, the **regular plural** masculine and feminine ending, as for adjectives, is **iin**,
eg m3allim[teacher] > m3allm**iin**[teachers]

b. **iyye** is used for the feminine when the masculine, oddly, ends in **e** (normally a feminine ending)
eg *lawyer* mu7aame[m] > mu7am**iyye**[f] (like for nationalities).

REMINDER When you add a suffix, remove the short vowel of the preceding syllable.
eg when you add to m3allim the feminine **e**, remove the **i** of lim: ~~m3allime~~ m3allme.

Occupation	Masculine	Feminine	Plural
Teacher	m3allim	m3allm**e**	m3allm**iin**
Artist	finneen	...	...
Engineer	mhandis	...	...
Nurse	mmarriD	mmarr**Da**	mmarr**Diin**
Cook	Tibbaakh	...	...
Hairdresser	7illaa2	...	...
Lawyer	mu7aame	mu7am**iyye**[as for nationality]	mu7amiyy**e**
Singer	mghanne	...	...

5.3 Say what the person does: eg cook[m] > **2ana Tibbaakh** (Choose from: 2ana / ni7na)
  1 engineer[m]   2 nurse[f]   3 lawyers   4 artist[m]   5 singer[f]   6 hairdressers

5.4 Find-aaword: Find the 5 professions, in spoken and standard.

b	i	m	3	a	l	l	i	m	m
n	b	l	f	i	n	n	ee	n	r
m	m	a	r	r	i	D	r	a	n
ee	k	aa	T	i	b	b	aa	k	h
m	u	7	aa	m	e	a	y	e	i

UNIT 5

GRAMMAR

PRESENT TENSE

 5.5 Complete the table:

REMINDER

a. The artificial **i** in the prefix is only there to break up the consonantal cluster.
b. If a word has more than one syllable, when you add a suffix, drop the preceding short vowel
   eg 2ana bishti**ghil**, but 2inte btishti**ghle**.

Person	Pronoun	Prefix	Stem	Suffix	Px	Stem	Sx	Px	Stem	Sx
			work			play			give	
1st	2ana	bi	shtighil		...	l3ab		...	a3Te	
	ni7na	mni	shtighil		...	...		...	...	
2nd	2inta	bti	shtighil		...	...		...	...	
	2inte	bti	shtighl	e	...	...	...	...	...	...
	2into	bti	shtighl	o	...	...	...	...	...	...
3rd	huwwe	byi	shtighil		...	...		...	...	
	hiyye	bti	shtighil		...	...		...	...	
	hinne	byi	shtighl	o	...	...	...	...	...	...

 5.6 Match the verb with the rest of the sentence eg bishtighil ka[as a] m3allim

1 btishtighle 2 mnil3ab 3 ma[doesn't] bta3Te 4 bit3allam[learn] 5 byishtighlo 6 byishtighil

a ka Tibbaakha b 3arabe c faTbool d ka mu7ame e ra2m talifoona f ka mhandsiin

 5.7 Ask: eg you[m] | cook > **shu btishtighil?**

1 they   2 she   3 you[m]   4 we   5 you[p]   6 you[f]

 5.8 Say what the person does: eg bishtighil | cook > **bishtighil ka Tibbaakh**

1 btishtighlo | teachers   2 btishtighil[she] | artist   3 btishtighil[you] | engineer
4 mnishtighil | lawyers   5 btishtighle | nurse   6 btishtighlo | singers

UNIT 5

COMPREHEND & COMMUNICATE

 5.9 tsamma3o[listen] w 7iTTo[put] X bi l3amuud[column] lmaZbuuT[correct]:

	a	b	c	d	e	f	g
Sa7							
ghalaT							

 5.10

su2aal[2as2ile]	jaweeb[2ajwibe]
shu **btishtighil**?	2ana **Tibbaakh** / bishtighil ka Tibbaakh

5.11 tbeedalo[exchange]: Find out what a couple of other (real or imaginary) individuals do for a living.

5.12 Read the note below and prepare a **sketch** with a:

    beginning (greetings/scene setting)

    middle   (problem) eg One person lies about their name, how they're feeling and their job.

    end   (resolution) eg Another person exposes them.

NOTE 5.12   **mish** + adjective eg hayda[m\e[f\ool[p]] **mish** 7ilo[m]\we[f]\wiin[p]   *This (is) / these (are)* ***not*** *beautiful*

                    + noun   eg hayda **mish** beet   *This is* ***not*** *a house*

           ma + verb   eg **ma** ba3Te 3inweene   *I* ***don't*** *give my address*

5.13 t7addaso[Converse] (tzakkaro[recall] l2as2ile[questions] w l2ajwibe[answers]):

    1 greetings **2** feeling **3** nationality **4** address | phone no. **5 occupation**

UNIT 6
Do you come from a large family?

DIALOGUE

1 greetings | name   2 feeling   3 nationality   4 address | phone no.   5 occupation   6 family   7 cafe   8 past activities   9 future activities   10 time | date | activity now   11 places | transport | directions   12 hotel   13 restaurant   14 shopping   15 pastimes | taste   16 tourism | weather

samiir w layla

1 S Sabaa7 lkheer, layla. nshalla mnii7a lyoom?
2 L 2e, ktiir mnii7a, nishkur 2alla^{God be praised}.
3 S layla, 2inte min 3ayle^{family} kbiire^{big} 2aw zghiire^{small}?
4 L 2ana min 3ayle kbiire. 3inde^{I have} tleet 2ikhwe^{brothers} w khams 2ikhweet^{sisters}, w 2inta?
5 S 2ana min 3ayle zghiire.
6 L kam^{how many} khayy^{brother} w 2ikht^{sister} 3indak?
7 S 3inde bas^{just} khayy w 2ikhteen. w 2into killkun^{all}   seekniin bi zeet^{same} lbeet?
8 L 2e, Tab3an^{of course}.
9 S w shu 3inween 2ikhiwtik^{siblings}?
10 L bi3tizir, ya mal3uun!^{oh crafty one!} |ma ra7 2a3Tiik|^{I won't give you} 3inween baytna ba3d^{yet}.
11 S Tayyib , ma3leesh. barke 2ariiban^{soon}.
12 L bkhaaTrak, samiir.
13 S ma3 i ssaleeme, layla. sallme ^{say hello} 3a ^{to} lkill^{everyone}.

1 Good morning, Layla. I hope you're well today.
2 Yes, very well, God be praised.
3 Layla, are you from a large or a small family?
4 I'm from a large family. I have three brothers and five sisters, and you?
5 I'm from a small family.
6 How many brothers and sisters do you have?
7 I have just one brother and two sisters. And are you all living in the same house?
8 Yes, of course.
9 And what's your siblings' address?
10 Sorry, you're such a sneak! I won't give you our house's address yet.
11 Ok, never mind. Maybe soon.
12 Bye, Samir
13 Bye, Layla. Give my regards to everyone.

 6.1

1 kiifa layla lyoom?
2 layla min 3ayle kbiire 2aw zghiire?
3 kam khayy w 2ikht 3inda?
4 samiir min 3ayle kbiire?
5 kam khayy w 2ikht 3indo?
6 ween^{where} sekniin kill 2ikhwit layla?

UNIT 6

CULTURE

FAMILY RELATIONS

Lebanese culture has personal relations at its heart. Family provides the pulse and the hearth from which all other interactions stem. Ties are very close. Grandparents, aunts and uncles along with other extended family members often play a central part in children's lives. They can rival each other to dispense loving care and pose as supplementary role models. For that reason, it is not so common to live beyond a coffee's throw away from other family members if that can be helped. Happy moments bring jubilation to all, while the burden of tragedy is also shared by the many.

VOCABULARY

FAMILY

 6.2 Follow the given bold-type endings to complete the table:

Family member	Singular	Dual	Plural
Family	3ayle	3ayilt**een**	3iyal
Child	walad	walad**een**	wleed
Brother	khayy / 2akh	khayy...	2ikhwe
Sister	2ikht	2ikht...	2ikhw**eet**
Father	bayy / 2ab	bayy...	2abaw...
Mother	2imm	2imm...	2imm...
Grandmother	sitt	sitt...	sitt...
Grandfather	jidd	jidd...	jduud

 6.3 Find-a-word: Find the same three family members, in both spoken and standard.

b	i	m	v	a	l	2	i	m	m
n	2	m	k	h	a	y	y	n	r
m	m	2	i	k	h	t	r	a	n

SIZE ADJECTIVES

 6.4 Follow the given bold-type endings to complete the table, after reading the note:

Adjective	Masculine	Feminine & plural of things
Large	kbiir	kbii**re**
Small	zghiir	zghiir...
Medium	mitwassiT	mitwassT...
Only (child)	wa7iid	wa7iid...

NOTE 6.4 For things, the plural is the same as the feminine singular.
eg 3ayle kbiire (fem. sg.)
   3iyal kbiire (plural)

 6.5 Ask & answer: you^m | tmeen 2ikhwe > **2inta** min 3ayle kbiire? **2e**, 2ana min 3ayle **kbiire**.
(Choose: 2e^{yes} | la2^{no})

1 they | khayy waa7ad. 2 we | 2arba3 2ikhwe. 3 you^p | 3ashr 2ikhwe.
4 she | 2ikhteen. 5 you^f | wa7iide. 6 he | walad waa7ad.

UNIT 6

GRAMMAR

NUMBER + NOUN

6.6 Read the rule and note below and complete the following number patterns:

RULE 6.6 (a) For **3 to 10** the noun that follows is **plural** (for vowel dropping at end of a number see 4.2)

    khayy (waa7ad)   khayyeen   tleet 2**ikhwe**   2arba3 2ikhwe ...

    2ikht (wi7de)   2ikhteen   tleet 2ikhweet   2arba3 2ikhweet ...

(b) From **11 upward** the noun that follows is **singular**.

NOTE 6.6 Add **ar** to numbers 11 to 19, eg 7da3sh**ar**, before a noun.

7da3sh**ar khayy/2ikht**   tna3shar khayy/2ikht   tletta3shar khayy/2ikht ...

wa7d**aw** 3ishriin **khayy/2ikht**   tneenaw 3ishriin khayy/2ikht ...

6.7 Ask & answer: you[m] | 3 brothers + 5 sisters >

    kam khayy w 2ikht 3indak[e\na...]? 3inde **tleet** 2ikhwe w khams 2ikhweet.

NOTE 6.7 Kam is followed by a singular noun.

1 they | 1 sister.	2 we | 3 brothers and 6 sisters.	3 you[p] | 13 brothers.
4 she | 2 brothers.	5 you[f] | only child.	6 he | 15 sisters.

SUN LETTERS

Sun letters are:

    d D,   s S,   t T,   l,   n,   r,   sh,   z

To help you remember: **z**oo **r**u**sh** **d**u**st**/**D**u**ST** **l**a**n**e (ignore vowels).

All other letters are **moon letters**.

The definite article "the" is expressed with "l" at the beginning of a word starting with a moon letter

    eg lfinneen[the artist], lmu7aame[the lawyer], lim3allim[the teacher].

But in a word starting with a sunletter, the sunletter is doubled, so that the first of the double replaces "l"

    eg TTibaakh[the cook], ssiyyaara[the car], SSiin[[the]China]

6.8 How do we say 'the' in the following words:

    1 3inween   2 sheeri3   3 ra2m   4 m3allim   5 see3a[watch]   6 shighil[work]

UNIT 6

COMPREHEND & COMMUNICATE

21

 6.9 tsamma3o[listen] w 7iTTo[put] X bi l3amuud[column] lmaZbuuT[correct]:

	a	b	c	d	e	f	g
Sa7							
ghalaT							

 6.10

su2aal[2as2ile]	jaweeb[2ajwibe]
2inta min 3ayle kbiire?	2e, 2ana min 3ayle **kbiire**.
kam khayy w 2ikht 3ind**ak**?	3ind**e tleet 2ikhwe** w **2arba3 2ikhweet**.

 6.11 tbeedalo[exchange]: Find out whether a couple of other (real or imaginary) individuals:
- come from a large family and
- how many brothers and sisters they have.

6.12 Prepare a **sketch** with a:
   beginning (greetings/scene setting)
   middle   (problem)   eg Someone gets the number of siblings wrong.
   end   (resolution) eg They apologise , say it is wrong, and correct the mistake.

6.13 t7addaso (tzakkaro l2as2ile w l2ajwibe):
   1 greetings **2** feeling **3** nationality **4** address | phone no. **5** occupation **6 family**

UNIT 7
Can I have a sandwich and a coke, please?

DIALOGUE

1 greetings | name 2 feeling 3 nationality 4 address | phone no. 5 occupation 6 family **7 cafe** 8 past activities 9 future activities
10 time | date | activity now 11 places | transport | directions 12 hotel 13 restaurant 14 shopping 15 pastimes | taste 16 tourism | weather

Layla, Samir & waiter

1 L   masa lkheer, samiir. kiifak?
2 S |meeshe l7aal|[fine]. tfaDDale[please] 23ide[sit down].
3 L   7ilwe[beautiful] ¹ha[this] l2ahwe[cafe], samiir. zaw2ak[taste] 7ilo[good].
4 S   shukran, layla. shu bit7ibbe[would you like] teekle[to eat] w tishrabe[to drink]?
5 L   finjeen[cup] 2ahwe[coffee] w saandwish faleefil, |3mool ma3ruuf|[if you please].
6 S   w 2ana badde[want] 2iT3it[piece] ba2leewa[baklava] w 2anniinit[bottle] koola[coke]. ra7[I will] |3ayyiT la|[call] rrijeel[man].
7 L   Tayyib[ok] 2inta Tloob[order] w 2ana bruu7 3a[go to] l7immeem[bathroom].
8 S   ya m3allim[sir], baddna[we want] saandwish faleefil, 2iT3it ba2leewa, waa7ad 2ahwe w ²wi7de[one] koola. b2addeesh[how much] byiTla3o[do they come to], |2iza bitriid|[if you please]?
9 W   tikram[sure], |byiTla3o bi| 3ishriin dolar.
10 S tfaDDal[here you are]. haay[here's] khamsaw 3ishriin dolar. [layla returns] w khalliilak[keep] lbee2e[the change].
11 L |shu kariim|[how generous] 2inta ya samiir! w shu 7ilwe ha lmanTa2a[area]!
12 S 2inte seekne |2ariib min|[close to] hoon, layla?
13 L |3a mahlak|[slow down], samiir. halla2 bas baddna nishrab[drink] w neekul[eat].
14 S bi3tizir, layla, |3ala raa7tik|[at your leisure] lakeen[in that case].

¹short for hayda/e/ool   ²feminine

1 Good evening, Samir. How are you?
2 Fine. Please, sit down.
3 This cafe is nice, Samir. You have good taste.
4 Thanks, Layla. What would you like to eat and drink?
5 A cup of coffee and a falafel sandwich, please.
6 And I want a piece of baklava and a bottle of coke. I'll call the guy.
7 Ok. You order and I'll go to the bathroom.
8 Hey, Young Man, we'd like a falafel sandwich, a piece of baklava, a coffee, and a coke. How much will that be, please?
9 Sure, that'll be twenty dollars.
10 Here you are, twenty-five dollars [Layla returns] and keep the change.
11 You're so generous, Samir! and what a beautiful area!
12 Do you live near here, Layla?
13 Slow down, Samir. Now we just want to drink and eat.
14 Sorry, Layla, as you please then.

 7.1

1 kiifo samiir lyoom?
2 kiif l2ahwe?
3 shu byiTlub samiir la[for] layla?
4 shu byiTlub 2ilo[for himself]?
5 b2addeesh byiTla3o?
6 samiir bakhiil[stingy]? la2, ...

UNIT 7

CULTURE
THE COFFEE RITUAL

The Lebanese are in general very generous. There is usually a race when a bill arrives as to who will be quicker to pay. They take great pleasure in beating you to it, even when you think it is a big amount. It is their way of showing their appreciation of your company.

One Lebanese visiting another is likely to refuse a coffee offer twice, saying they do not want to trouble the host. The third time they usually acquiesce. The visitor may also leave a small residue in their cup or on their food plate as a show of noble satisfaction or lack of greed.

It is not rare to find one's coffee cup tipped when finished, and for someone to read the fortune it brings, with added spice, drama and even advice.

VOCABULARY

FOOD 2akl	
falafel sandwich	saandwish[eet] faleefil
cheese/salad/chicken	jibne / slaaTa / djeej
piece of cake	2iT3it[2iTa3] 7ilo

DRINK mashruub[eet]	
cup of tea	finjeen[fnejiin] shaay
bottle of Fanta	2anniinit[2aneene] fanta
can of Coke	tankit[tankeet] / 3ilbit[3ilab] koola
a glass of orange juice / apple / pear / berry	kibbeeyit[kibbeyeet] 3aSiir lbird2aan / ttiffee7 / nnjaaS / ttuut
breakfast / lunch / dinner	tirwii2a / ghada / 3asha

NOTE 7.2 For **nouns** referring to **non-humans**, the masculine and feminine **regular plural** ending is **eet**. Irregular plurals become familiar through general reading.

REMINDER The feminine **a/e** ending turns into **it** where **of** can be used in English eg 2anniine, but 2anniinit[of] kola.

7.2 Circle the word that does not fit in the series:
    1 2anniine|tanke|saandwish|kibbeeye. **2** tuut|shaay|tiffee7|njaaS. **3** jibne|7ilo|slaaTa|djeej.
    4 ghada|2akl|3asha|tirwii2a.

7.3 Order: eg cheese sandwich > **saandwish jibne**, 3mool ma3ruuf.
    1 chicken sandwich.   2 can of coke and a piece of baklava.   3 two cups of coffee.
    4 glass of apple juice.   5 three pieces of cake.   6 four cups of tea.

GRAMMAR
THE ARTICLE (A / THE)

7.4 Complete the table: (**NOTE 7.4:** The adjective comes last. What belongs comes first).

RULE 7.4

a	↓↓	beeb kbiir [A big door]	A fast car	siyyaara sarii3a
the	11	lbeeb likbiir [The big door]	The fast car	...
is	1↓	lbeeb kbiir [The door is small]	The car **is** fast	...
's/of	↓1	beeb lghirfe [The door of the room]	The mother's car	siyyaarit l2imm
your	↓↓	beeb ghirfitna [The door of our room]	Your mother's car	...
your	↓↓1	beeb ghirfitna likbiir [The big door of our room]	Your mother's fast car	...

UNIT 7

 7.5 Match the numbers with the letters:

1 a small family	a 3aylit m3allmak	1 a great artist	a stuudyo finneenak	1 a tired child	a li3bit waladak
2 the small family	b 3ayle zghiire	2 the great artist	b listuudyo kbiir	2 the tired child	b li3bit lwalad
3 the family is small	c l3ayle lizghiire	3 the studio is big	c lfinnen likbiir	3 the child is tired	c lwalad ti3been
4 the teacher's family	d 3aylit lim3allim	4 the artist's studio	d stuudyo lfinneen	4 the child's toy	d lwalad tti3been
5 your teacher's family	e l3ayle zghiire	5 your artist's studio	e finneen kbiir	5 your[m] child's toy	e walad ti3been

7.6 Complete with what's in brackets? eg shu fi[there is] bi lgaraaj? fi (a car) > fi **siyyaara**.
  1 shu fi bi lijnayne[garden]? fi (a tree[shajra])
  2 shu hayde[this]? hayde (a big tree)
  3 ween[where] (the big tree)?
  4 |la miin|[whose] hayde shshajra? hayde (your[m] mother's tree)
  5 kiif[how] (the tree? The tree is big)
  6 shu fi bi lijnayne? fi (your mother's big tree)

THE PRESENT TENSE

7.7 After reading the notes, rules and reminders below, complete the following table:

	b followed by **vowel**											b followed by **consonant**								
	P[refix]	Stem	S[uffix]	P	Stem	S	P	Stem	S	P	Stem	S	P	Stem	S	P	Stem	S	P	Stem	S
Pronoun	drink			[bill]come to/go up			eat			take			would like						(will) be		
2ana	bi	shrab		...	Tla3[bi]		b	eekul		...	eekhud		b	7ibb		...	riid		...	kuun	
ni7na	mni	shrab		...	...		mn	eekul		...	...		min	7ibb		...	...		...	...	
2inta	bti	shrab		...	...		bt	eekul		...	...		bit	7ibb		...	...		...	...	
2inte	bti	shrab	e	...	...		bt	eekul	e	...	...		bit	7ibb	...	...	...		...	...	...
2into	bti	shrab	o	...	...		bt	eekul	o	...	...		bit	7ibb	...	...	...		...	...	...
huwwe	byi	shrab		...	...		by	eekul		...	...		bi	7ibb		...	...		...	...	
hiyye	bti	shrab		...	...		bt	eekul		...	...		bit	7ibb		...	...		...	...	
hinne	byi	shrab	o	...	...		by	eekul	o	...	...		bi	7ibb	...	...	...		...	...	...

NOTE 7.7 The P[refix] and S[uffix] change, but the S[tem] remains mostly the same.
REMINDER Where needed, the **i** shifts according to the consonant cluster rule of counting two from the back.
If the stem has more than one vowel, drop its last short vowel when you add a suffix.
If you are left with a consonant cluster, use **i**.
RULE 7.7 Look at the first person, if **b** is followed by a **vowel**, **by** is used in the third person (except for hiyye)
if **b** is followed by a **consonant**, **bi** is used in the third person

7.8 Look at the first column and circle the three pronouns whose verb takes the vowel suffix: **e** or **o**?

7.9 Look at the first person as your guide and decide if **bi or by** is needed in the third person:
  2ana   1 bishrab   2 b7ibb   3 ba3Te   4 beekhud   5 bruu7[go]
  huwwe   a ...   b ...   c ....   d ...   e ...

7.10 Given the consonant cluster rule and looking at the first person in the above exercise, decide if:
  bt/bit/bti is needed for the second person:
  2inta   a ...   b ...   c ....   d ...   e ...

7.11 Ask: eg leesh[why] (you[m] eat) ktiir? > leesh **bteekul** ktiir?
1 shu (he drinks) SSib7[in the morning]?
2 shu (they eat) |3a lghada|[for lunch]?
3 (You[p] take) maasterkard?
4 leesh (you[f] take) tankit koola lghaalye[expensive] badel[rather than] lirkhiiSa[cheap]?
5 ween[where] (he will be) bukra[tomorrow] bi ha[this] lwa2t[time]?
6 b2addeesh[how much] (they come to) l2ahwe w shshaay?

7.12 Answer to order: eg shu bit7ibb? ... sandwish djeej. > **beekhud** saandwish djeej, min faDlak.
  eg shu bit7ibb[e\o]/bitriid[e\o] bteekhud[e\o]? In your answer you would use **beekhud**[mneekhud \ bteekhud ...]
NOTE 7.12 **bit7ibb** and **bitriid** are the polite way for the waiter to ask for what you would like,

  1 shu bitriide? ... finjeen shaay.
  2 shu bteekhdo? ... tankit koola.
  3 shu bit7ibb? ... 2iT3it 7ilo.
  4 shu bitriido? ... tleet fnejiin 2ahwe.
  5 shu bit7ibb? ... saandwish jibne.
  6 shu bitriide? ... 2anniinit 3aSiir.

UNIT 7

NEGATING THE PRESENT

RULE 7.13 To negate the present place **ma** before the verb eg beekul *I eat.* **ma** beekul *I don't eat.*

7.13 Negate: eg btishrab 2ahwe SSib7? | lmasa > la2, **ma bishrab** 2ahwe SSib7, bishrab 2ahwe lmasa.
1 bteekul ktiir SSib7? | lmasa.   3 byishtighlo ka Tibbakhiin? | m3allmiin.   5 bteekhud finjeen 2ahwe? | shaay.
2 baddo saandwish jibne? | faleefil. 4 bukra bitkuun^m bi bayruut? | lQaahira^cairo. 6 bta3Te ra2m talifoona? | ra2m bayta

7.14   Choose between **ma or mish** (**REMINDER** *mish is used to negate nouns and adjectives*).
               eg **baddak** 2anniinit koola? | tankit fanta > la2, **ma badde** 2anniinit koola, badde tankit fanta.
1 baddo saandwish faleefil? | jibne   3 btishrabo koola? | 3aSiir   5 l7eeT^wall 3ariiD^wide ? | dayyi2^narrow
2 hayde 2anniine? | tanke   4 hayde ssiyyaara 7ilwe? | bish3a^ugly   6 byiTlub biira? wiski

AUXILIARY/TO/ADVERBS OF TIME + PRESENT

RULE 7.15
(a) After: **modals**^words accompanying verb   eg **fiine**^can, **leezim**^should, **bSiir**^develop the habit of / become
          to   eg **badde**^want to, **ra7**^going to, **b7ibb**^like to, **la/ta**^(in order) to
          adverbs of time   eg **7atta**^until, **2abilma**^before, **ba3idma**^after
  the beginning **b** and **m** of the present tense are dropped,
               eg fiine ~~b~~ruu7? baddna ~~m~~neekul. byeekhud maSaare^money ta^to ~~b~~yidfa3^pay.
(b) All Arabic syllables, including the first, must start with a consonant (see below).
  When the *b* of the: **1st person** that is followed by a vowel is dropped, it is replaced with **2**.
               eg fiine ~~b~~2ishrab? badde ~~b~~2eekul.
          3rd person is dropped (except for the feminine), it is replaced with **y**.
               eg fi ~~bi~~ykuun^he can be. baddun ~~bi~~yruu7o^they want to go. ma ra7 ~~bi~~y7ibbo l2akl^they're not going to like the food.

7.15 Ask: eg shu baddak (bteekul)? > shu **baddak teekul**?
1 2ayya^which lighgha^language fiik^can you (bti7ke^speak)?   4 bit7ibb (bteekul) buuZa^icecream?
2 leesh ra7 (bitruu7^go)?   5 leesh ma bi7ibbo (byeeklo) ktiir 2abilma (bineemo^sleep)?
3 miin^who leezim (byidfa3) lfetuura^bill?   6 ra7 (mna3Te) rrijeel bakhshiish^tip 2aw^or la2?

THE IMPERATIVE^order/instruction

7.16 Use the following verbs as future models and to complete this table:

RULE 7.16a To form the imperative, **drop the prefix** of the second person of the present:

PRESENT	IMPERATIVE		
2inta	MASCULINE	FEMININE	PLURAL
bit7ibb^like/love	~~bit~~7ibb	~~bit~~7ibbe	~~bit~~7ibbo
bitruu7^go	...	...	...
bitfuut^enter	...	...	...
bitjiib^bring	...	...	...
btitfaDDal^here you are/invite sone to do sthg	...	...	...
btitTalla3^look	...	...	...

RULE 7.16b If the verb doesn't have a long vowel or double letter, make the **masculine vowel long**:

mid a	btishrab^drink	~~bti~~shraab	~~bti~~shrabe	~~bti~~shrabo
	btiw2af^stop/stand	...	...	...
mid u	bteekul^eat	~~bt~~eekool	kile	kilo
	bta3mul^do	~~bta~~3mool	3mile	3milo
end a	bti2ra^read	~~bti~~2raa	2ri	2ru
	btighfa^fall asleep	...	...	...
end e	btishitre^buy	~~bti~~shtrii	shtri	shtru
	bta3Te^give	~~bta~~3Tii	...	...

a > aa   u > oo   end e > ii   all > i excp a   all > i excp a & end e > u

UNIT 7

HOW TO MAKE AN OMELETTE

7.17 Use the imperative for the recipe^{waSfe} eg (^mbtishitre) lmukawwineet^{ingredients} > **shtrii** lmukawwineet
1 (^mbit7amme^{heat up}) zibde^{butter} bi mi2leeye^{frypan}. 6 (^fbtiksur^{break}) beeD^{eggs} 3a^{over} ttuum.
2 (^mbit2aTTi3^{cut up}) baTaaTa^{potatoes}. 7 (^pbtikhluT^{mix in}) ma3un ba2duunis^{parsley} w baSal^{onion} m2aTTa3^{cut up}.
3 (^mbit7iTT^{place}) lbaTaaTa bi lmi2leeye. 8 (^pbitDiif^{add}) mil7^{salt} w bhaar^{pepper}.
4 (^fbitdi22^{crush}) shwayyit^{a bit of} tuum^{garlic}. 9 (^pbitkitt^{pour}) lkhaliiT^{mixture} foo2^{over} lbaTaaTa.
5 (^fbit7iTT) ttuum bi |Sa7n ghamii2|^{bowl}. 10 ba3d shwayy (^pbti2lub^{turn over}) |kill shi|^{everything}.

POLITE REQUESTS

7.18 Complete the table:

Please		Masculine	Feminine	Plural
	Verb	2iza bitrii**d** / law sama7**t**	...	...
	Possessive ending	min faDl**ak**	...	...
	Imperative	**3mool** ma3ruuf	...	...

NEGATING THE IMPERATIVE

RULE 7.19 To negate the imperative, place ma before the 2nd person of the present and remove the prefix b.
  eg present: bteekul/bteekle/bteeklo *you eat*^{mfp}   imperative: ma ~~b~~teekul/~~b~~teekle/~~b~~teeklo

7.19 Give the person advice eg 2ana shib3aan^{full}. ma (bteekul) > **ma teekul** lakeen^{then}.
 1 2ana mish ti3been, ma (bti23ud^{sit down}).   4 ni7na mish 3iTshaniin^{thirsty}, ma (btishrab).
 2 2ana mish mista3ijle^{in a hurry}, ma (btisra3^{speed}). 5 2ana mish ju3aane^{hungry}, ma (bteekul).
 3 ni7na mish ni3seniin^{sleepy}, ma (bitneem^{sleep}). 6 ni7na ma min7ibb nitruk^{leave} lbeet, ma (bitseefir^{travel}).

COMPREHEND & COMMUNICATE

7.20 tsamma3o w 7iTTo X bi l3amuud lmaZbuuT:

	a	b	c	d	e	f
Sa7						
ghalaT						

 7.21 ghayyro^{change} lkalimeet^{words} yalle^{which} |b khaTT ghaami2|^{bold type}:

2as2ile	2ajwibe
shu **bit7ibb teekul**?	beekhud saandwish faleefil, **3mool ma3ruuf**.
baddak tishrab shi^{something}?	**2e, 2anniinit biira** / la2, ma badde 2ishrab shi^{anything}, bas saandwish djeej, 2iza bitriid.
b2addeesh **byiTla3o**?	byiTla3o bi **khams** dolaraat.

7.22 tbeedalo: Find out what a couple of other (real or imaginary) individuals would order if they were in a cafe now, using Table 7.2 as a menu.

 7.23 Prepare a **sketch** with a:
 beginning (greetings/scene setting)
 middle (problem) eg the food is not good/the waiter gets the wrong order/ gives back the wrong change.
 end (resolution)

 7.24 t7addaso (tzakkaro l2as2ile w l2ajwibe):
 1 greetings **2** feeling **3** nationality **4** address | phone no. **5** occupation **6** family **7 cafe**

UNIT 8
What did you do last weekend?

DIALOGUE

1 greetings | name 2 feeling 3 nationality 4 address | phone no. 5 occupation 6 family 7 cafe **8 past activities** 9 future activities
10 time | date | activity now 11 places | transport | directions 12 hotel 13 restaurant 14 shopping 15 pastimes | taste 16 tourism | weather

samiir w layla

1 L Sabaa7 lkheer, samiir. nshalla mnii7?
2 S 2ana ktiir mabSuuT^{happy} lyoom.
3 L leesh^{why} mabSuuT?
4 S li2anne^{because} 2aDDayt^{spent} |niheeyit 2usbuu3|^{weekend} ktiir 7ilwe.
5 L leesh shu 3milt$^{did\ you\ do}$?
6 S |yoom ssabt|$^{on\ Saturday}$ SSib7$^{in\ the\ morning}$, trawwa2t$^{I\ had\ [for]\ breakfast}$ mne2iish$^{herb\ pizza}$. |ba3d DDohr|$^{in\ the\ afternoon}$, l3ibt$^{I\ played}$ faTbool. w lmasa$^{in\ the\ evening}$, |ri7t 3a|$^{I\ went\ to}$ ssinama ma3^{with} 2aSdiQaa2e^{friends}. w l2a7ad ^{Sunday} rta7t$^{I\ rested}$ kill^{all} nnhaar^{day}. w 2inte shu 3milte?
7 L 2ana |ntabaht la|$^{looked\ after}$ 2imme ssabt w l2a7ad |2akhadta 3a|$^{I\ took\ her\ to}$ lmistashfa^{hospital} li2anna$^{because\ she}$ keenit^{was} mariiDa^{sick}.
8 S w kiifa halla2?
9 L Saarit$^{she\ has\ become}$ 2a7san, nishkur 2alla.
10 S layla, 2into seekniin |b3aad 3an|$^{far\ from}$ lmistashfa?
11 L la2, ni7na seekniin bi sheeri3 lmistashfa.
12 S ra2m lmistashfa wa7daw khamsiin. w 2into, ra2m baytkun foo2^{above} 2aw^{or} ta7t^{below} lkhamsiin?
13 L ni7na ra2imna been^{between} khamsiin w 2alf.
14 S 2ana ktiir b7ibb 2itmashsha$^{going\ for\ a\ walk}$ bi sheeri3kun. yimkin^{maybe} shuufik$^{I\ see\ you}$ huniik |shi yoom|$^{one\ day}$.

1 Good morning, Samir. I hope you're well?
2 I'm very happy today.
3 Why are you happy?
4 Because I had a very nice weekend.
5 Why what did you do?
6 On Saturday morning, I had a herb pizza for breakfast. In the afternoon, I played football. In the evening, I went to the cinema with my friends. On Sunday, I rested all day. And you, what did you do?
7 I looked after my mother Saturday and on Sunday I took her to hospital because she was sick.
8 And how is she now?
9 She's better, thank you.
10 Layla, do you live far from the hospital?
11 No, we live in the same street as the hospital.
12 The hospital's number is 51. And you, your house number, is it above or below fifty?
13 Our number is between fifty and one thousand.
14 I really enjoy going for walks in your street. I might see you there one day.

8.1

1 kiifo samiir lyoom?
2 kiif keenit niheeyit 2usbuu3o?
3 shu 2aal^{said} samiir 3imil^{did} yoom ssabt SSib7? 2aal: "...."
4 shu 2aalit layla 3imlit nhaar ssabt? 2aalit "...."
5 ween seekne layla?
6 shu 2aal samiir bya3mul bisheeri3 layla? 2aal: "...."

UNIT 8

CULTURE

LIFESTYLE

Most of the Lebanese have two homes, one in the city and another up in the mountains for a quick weekend getaway and a cool retreat in the summer. Apart from the spectacular views, being high up also offers the tranquillity of a haven from the bustle of the city, skiing in the winter, and cosy temperatures in the summer. Given the compact size of the country(10,400 km^2), people can ski in the morning and swim in the Mediterranean in the afternoon in spring and autumn.

People's main activities tend to be socialising, going for a stroll, and watching the news, soaps and variety shows.

Young people favour playing soccer, basketball, table tennis, windsurfing and kayaking. Older women cook, knit, crochet and may be caught gossiping over a coffee sip.

VOCABULARY

WHAT DID YOU DO LAST WEEK(END)?

	l7aaDir^{present}	lmaaDe^{past}
shu 3milt$^{e/o}$ bi |niheeyit^{end} l2usbuu3^{week}| ^{weekend}? l2usbuu3 lmaaDe^{last}?	ba3mul	3milt
2akalt^{ate} ktiir	beekul	2akalt
ttaSalt^{contacted} bi ^{friend}Sadii2e$^{te \setminus 2aSdiQaa2e}$	bittiSil	ttaSalt
3milt^{did} farDe^{homework}	ba3mul	3milt
shribt^{drank} 2ahwe ma3 2ikhte	bishrab	shribt
see3adt^{helped} jaare^{neighbour} bi nna2l$^{moving\ house}$	bsee3id	see3adt
l3ibt^{played} tenis / faTbool	bil3ab	l3ibt
2riit^{read} kteeb^{book} 7ilo^{enjoyable}	bi2ra	2riit
zirt^{visited} Sadii2e	bzuur	zirt
2ijeene$^{received\ visitor}$zeeyir^{zuwwaar}	byijiine	2ijeene
saba7t^{swam} bi lmasba7$^{swimming\ pool}$ / lba7r^{sea}	bisba7	saba7t
seefart^{travelled} 3a london	bseefir	seefart
kint^{was} bi lyabaan	bkuun	kint
shift^{saw} film	bshuuf	shift
tmashshayt$^{went\ for\ a\ walk}$ lawa7de^{alone}	bitmashsha	tmashshayt
^{went}ri7t 3a shshighil^{work}/ssuu2^{market}/lmaT3am^{restaurant}/l7adii2a^{park}	bruu7	ri7t
ri7t shtarayt kam gharaD$^{I\ went\ shopping}$	bishtre	shtarayt

 8.2 Answer the question genuinely eg **shu 3milt$^{e/o}$ bi niheeyit l2usbu3?** > **l3ibt faTabool**.
  1 ....   2 ....   3 ....   4 ....   5 ....   6 ....

GRAMMAR

PAST TENSE

8.3 Complete the following table:

	ate	contacted	swam	helped	travelled	went for a walk	bought
						ay	**> y dropped**
2ana	2akalt	ttaSalt	saba7t	see3adt	seefart[3a]	tmashshayt	shtarayt
ni7na	2akalna					tmashshayna	shtarayna
2inta	2akalt	...	...	...	...	...	...
2inte	2akalte	...	...	...	...	...	...
2into	2akalto	...	...	...	...	...	...
huwwe	2akal	...	...	...	...	tmashsha	...
hiyye	2akalit	...	...	...	...	tmashshit	...
hinne	2akalo	...	...	...	...	tmashsho	...

3rd person changes for verbs with:

	short i				**long ii**
	3 consonant root eg 3ml + i after 1st consonant			**2 consonant** root eg kh f i > ee/aa if guttural/r	> e / y
	did	drank	played	got scared	went	saw	was	read
	3milt	shribt	l3ibt	khift	ri7t[3a]	shift	kint	2riit
	3imil	shirib	li3ib	khaaf	raa7	sheef	keen	2ire
	...	...	...	...	...	...	...	2iryit
	...	...	...	...	...	...	...	2iryo

8.4 Ask: eg l2usbuu3 lmaaDe ri7t 3a London. > shu **3milt l2usbuu3 lmaaDe?**
1 l2usbuu3 lmaaDe saba7t[f] ma3 2aSdiQaa2e. 3 sheef film 7ilo l2usbuu3 lmaaDe. 5 seefarna 3a libneen ssine[year] lmaaDye (la ween ...?)
2 2akalit ktiir bi niheeyit l2usbuu3. 4 see3ado 2immun bi niheeyit l2usbuu3. 6 2iryit meeri kteeb 7ilo shshahr[month] lmaaDe.

8.5 Negate 1 to 6 in the above exercise:

RULE 8.5 Like for the present, **to negate the past** place **ma** before the verb eg **ma 2akalt** *I didn't eat.*

1 ....   2 ....   3 ....   4 ....   5 ....   6 ....

UNIT 8

COMPREHEND & COMMUNICATE

 8.6 tsamma3o w 7iTTo X bi l3amuud lmaZbuuT:

	a	b	c	d	e	f
Sa7						
ghalaT						

 8.7 What variations on the words in bold type can you think of?

su2aal	jaweeb
shu **3milt l2usbuu3 lmaaDe**?	**ri7t 3a ssinama** ma3 2ikhte.

 8.8 tbeedalo: Find out what a couple of other (real or imaginary) individuals did last week(end).

 8.9

Prepare a **sketch** with a:

beginning (greetings/scene setting)

middle (problem) eg Everything you did last week was totally different from the other person / others. You nearly conclude (**ma fiina nkuun 2aSdiQaa2**^{we can't be friends}) because you have nothing in common.

end (resolution) eg The last activity you mention proves to be a passion for both/all.

 8.10a t7addaso (tzakkaro l2as2ile w l2ajwibe):

1 greetings   **2** feeling   **3** nationality   **4** address | phone no.   **5** occupation   **6** family   **7** cafe   **8 past activities**

8.10b KEEP A **DAILY/WEEKLY DIARY** OF WHAT YOU'VE DONE.

UNIT 9
What are you going to do next weekend?

DIALOGUE

1 greetings | name 2 feeling 3 nationality 4 address | phone no. 5 occupation 6 family 7 cafe 8 past activities **9 future activities**
10 time | date | activity now 11 places | transport | directions 12 hotel 13 restaurant 14 shopping 15 pastimes | taste 16 tourism | weather

    samiir w layla

1 L   mar7aba, samiir.
2 S   2ahlan, layla.
3 L   shu, hayi2tak^{seem} ktiir mabSuuT lyoom.
4 S   leesh la2? niheeyit l2usbuu3 ljeey ra7$^{going\ to}$ 2a3mul 2ishya^{things} ktiir 7ilwe.
5 L   leesh 3am bitzarrikle$^{teasing\ me}$, samiir? bta3rif^{know} 2inno^{that} 2imme Saakhne w ra7 2inzirib$^{be\ stuck}$ bi lbeet.
6 S   bi3tizir, layla, nshalla 2immik tSiir mnii7a |bi sir3a|^{quickly}.
7 L   shukran, samiir, 3ala kalimeetak^{words} llaTiife^{kind}. lakeen^{so} 2inta shu ra7 ta3mul?
8 S |yoom ssabt|$^{on\ Saturday}$ SSib7, ra7 2itrawwa2 |fuul mdammas|$^{marinated\ beans}$. ba3d DDohr , ra7 ruu7 2isba7^{swim} ma3 Sadii2e kariim. w lmasa, ra7 2i7Dar^{see} film bi ssinama ma3 2ikhte saamya. w l2a7ad^{Sunday} ra7 2irtee7 kill nnhaar. w mitl^{like} l3aade^{usual}, ra7 |2itfarraj 3a|^{watch} lfaTbool 3a ttalfizyoon. w 2inte shu ra7 ta3mle?
9 L   ni7na 3aadatan^{usually} minruu7 3a ljabal^{mountain}, bas halla2 |ma fiina|$^{can't}$ li2anno 2imme Saakhne. leezim ninTur^{wait} ta^{until} tSi77^{recover}.
10 S   7araam$^{poor\ thing}$ 2immik, layla!
11 L   shukran samiir 3ala 2ihtimeemak^{concern}.
12 S   b7ibb kameen ruu7 shuufa w 2eekhidla zhuur^{flowers}.
13 L   yiy^{oh}! la2, la2, ma fiik. bta3mille mishikle^{problem}, samiir, li2anna ba3d^{still} ma bta3rif^{know} 3annak$^{about\ you}$.
14 S   w 2imtiin^{when} ra7 t2uliila$^{tell\ her}$?
15 L   mish bi ha ssir3a, samiir. ra7 2illa bi lwa2t^{time} limneesib^{suitable}, mish 2abl.

1 Hello, Samir.
2 Hi, Layla.
3 Why, you seem so happy today.
4 Why not? Next weekend, I'm going to do very nice things.
5 Why are you teasing me, Samir? You know my mother is sick and I'll be stuck at home.
6 Sorry, Layla. I hope your mother gets better quickly.
7 Thank you, Samir, for your kind words. So, what are you going to do?
8 On Saturday morning, I'm having marinated beans for breakfast. In the afternoon, I'm going swimming with my friend Karim. In the evening, I'm seeing a film with my sister Samya. On Sunday, I'm going to rest all day. As usual, I'll watch soccer on TV. And you, what are you going to do?
9 We usually go to [our house in] the mountains. But now we can't because Mum is sick. We have to wait till she recovers.
10 Poor thing your mother, Layla!
11 Thanks, Samir, for your concern.
12 I'd also like to go see her and take her flowers.
13 Oh! No! No! You can't. You'll create a problem for me, Samir, because she still doesn't know about you.
14 And when are you going to tell her?
15 Not so quickly, Samir. I'll tell her when the time is right, not before.

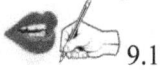 9.1

1 kiifo samiir lyoom?
2 miin^{who} bizarrik^{tease} la miin?
3 shu 2aal^{said} ra7 ya3mul yoom ssabt ba3d DDohr?
4 leesh layla ra7 tinzirib bi lbeet?
5 la ween bitruu7 3aylit layla 3aadatan bi niheeyit l2usbuu3?
6 la 2imtiin ra7 yiniTro?

UNIT 9

CULTURE

HEALTH CARE

Lebanon has three universities producing doctors who have to get through a stringent selection system, creating highly skilled general practitioners and specialised surgeons.

There are one hundred and thirty hospitals in Lebanon. The majority are private hospitals, with twenty hospitals belonging to the public sector. There is a major reliance on private insurance.

Treatment ranges from charity for the poor, to the wealthy spending hundreds of thousands on beauty therapies and plastic surgery.

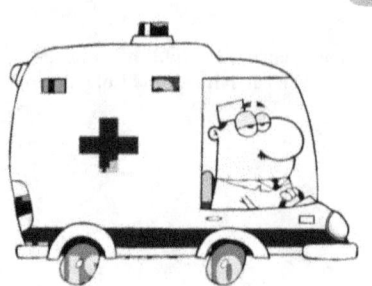

VOCABULARY

PLURAL OF ADJECTIVES

RULE 9.2a
For **things**, the regular plural ending, both masculine and feminine is **e/a**[after a guttural letter/r], as for the **feminine singular ending**.
    eg [f]madrase[school] kbiir**e** | madeeris[p] kbiir**e**   sheeri3[m] 3ariiD[wide] | shaweeri3[p] 3ariiD**a**.
For **people**, the regular plural ending, both masculine and feminine, is **iin**.
    eg [m]lim3allmiin[teachers] ti3ben**iin** / [f]lim3allmeet ti3ben**iin**.
Irregular patterns, such as those appearing in the table below, will become familiar with reading.

RULE 9.2b If the masculine adjective ends in: **o**, the o turns into **w**:   eg 7il**o**   7il**we**[f]   7il**wiin**[p]
If the masculine already ends in   **e**, the e turns into **iyye/iya** eg [rich]ghan**e**[m]   ghan**iyye**[f]   2aghn**iya**[p]

9.2 Follow the given major patterns to fill in the table below:
REMINDER When you make an addition to a word, remove the short vowel of the preceding syllable.

	Singular	[a]Plural	
		Things fem. = plural	**People** masc. & fem.
fast slow	sarii3 baTii2	sarii3a baTii2a	sari3iin baTi2iin
beautiful ugly	7ilo bishi3	7ilwe ...	7ilwiin ...
interesting boring	7ilo mumill	... ...	... ...
happy unhappy	mabSuuT ta3iis	... ...	... ...
a little a lot	2aliil ktiir	... ...	**ee (aa if guttural/ r)** 2leel ktaar
near far	2ariib b3iid	2ariibe b3iide	2raab b3aad
new old	jdiid 3atii2	... ...	... ...
long/tall short	Tawiil 2aSiir	... ...	[b]Twaal ...
clean dirty	nDiif wisikh	... ...	... wiskhiin
nice nasty	laTiif la2iim	... ...	**.u.a.a** luTafa lu2ama
generous stingy	kariim bakhiil	... ...	... ...
rich poor	ghane fa2iir	ghaniyye fa2iira	**.a..i.a** 2aghniya fu2ara
intelligent stupid	zake mahbuul	... mahbuule	... mhebiil

NOTE 9.2 a The above columns show that, officially, 'things' have different plurals from 'people', based on Standard Arabic, but in everyday speech people tend to blur that difference by often using them interchangeably.
    b In this section, words containing **S, D, T, Z** anywhere in the word take **aa** eg Twaal

UNIT 9

9.3 Ask: eg kutub > kiif **keenit lkutub**[books]? || wleed > kiif **keeno liwleed**[children]?
   1 2afleem[films]   2 byuut[houses]   3 m3allmiin   4 nees[people]   5 2leem[pens]   6 2aSdiQaa2

9.4 Describe: eg rriweeyeet[novels] keenit (long)   > rriweeyeet keenit **Tawiile**
                    liwleed keeno (tall)   > liwleed keeno **Twaal**

1 l2afleem keenit (not new)   3 lim3allmiin keeno (not very happy)   5 li2leem keenit (many)
2 libyuut keenit (very old)   4 nnees keno (a little nasty)   6 l2aSdiQaa2 keeno (few)

GRAMMAR

THE FUTURE

RULE 9.5 To form the future, place **ra7**[going to] before the present verb and **remove b/m** from the prefix.
REMINDER In Arabic every syllable must start with a consonant (see 7.15b). So,
- if after removing b/m, the following letter of the **1st person** is a vowel, add **2** to the beginning eg ra7 ~~b~~2eekul
- the **3rd person** must always start with **y** (except for 'hiyye') eg byeekul > ra7 yeekul || bisee3do[help]> ra7 ysee3ido

9.5 Change the tense of the following present verbs into the future (going to) in the table below:

PRESENT	beekul	[go]bruu7[3a]	bsee3id	bittiSil[bi]	bisba7	bseefir[3a]	ba3mul	bishrab	bil3ab	bi2ra
	FUTURE									
	ra7 ...									
2ana	**2**eekul	ruu7	see3id	...	...	...	...	...	...	...
ni7na	neekul	nruu7	nsee3id	...	...	...	...	...	...	...
2inta	teekul	truu7	tsee3id	...	...	...	...	...	...	...
2inte	teekle	truu7e	tsee3de	...	...	...	...	...	...	...
2into	teeklo	truu7o	tsee3do	...	...	...	...	...	...	...
huwwe	**y**eekul	yruu7	ysee3id	...	...	...	...	...	...	...
hiyye	teekul	truu7	tsee3id	...	...	...	...	...	...	...
hinne	**y**eeklo	yruu7o	ysee3do	...	...	...	...	...	...	...

9.6 Ask: eg 2inta | l2usbuu3 ljeey[next] > shu ra7 **ta3mul l2usbuu3** ljeey?
   1 huwwe | l2usbuu3 ljeey   3 hinne | bi niheeyit l2usbuu3 ljeey   5 2into | bi niheeyit l2usbuu3 ljeey
   2 ni7na | l2usbuu3 ljeey   4 hiyye | l2usbuu3 ljeey   6 2inte | bi niheeyit l2usbuu3 ljeey

9.7 Answer: eg shu ra7 ta3mul? (eat a lot) > ra7 **2eekul ktiir**.
   1 shu ra7 ta3mul? (help) jaare bi nna2l   4 shu ra7 ya3imlo? (drink) 2ahwe ma3 sittun.
   2 shu ra7 ta3imle? (contact) 2aSdiQaa2e   5 shu ra7 ta3imle? (read) kteeb ktiir 7ilo.
   3 shu ra7 na3mul? (do) fariDna   6 shu ra7 ta3mul? (travel to) maSr.

UNIT 9

THE NEGATIVE

RULE 9.8 To form the negative of the: **present & past**: use **ma** eg ma beekul ma 2akalt
 future: use **ma/mish** eg ma/mish ra7 2eekul

9.8 Turn the following verbs into past, present and future negatives. The first has been done for you.

	Past	present	future
2ana	ma 2akalt	ma beekul	ma/mish ra7 2eekul
ni7na	...	...	...
2inta	...	...	...
2inte	...	...	...
2into	...	...	...
huwwe	...	...	...
hiyye	...	...	...
hinne	...	...	...

9.9 Ask and say what the problem is: eg ra7 7ibb l2akl > shu lmishikle[problem]? **ma/mish ra7 7ibb l2akl**.
1 bitsee3id khayya bi shighlo.   3 2akal kill[whole] ssaandwish.   5 fiine 2a3mul farDe.
2 ttaSalo bi 2immun.   4 ra7 ni2dir[be able to] nruu7 ma3kun.   6 ra7 truu7 tisba7 ma3a.

COMPREHEND & COMMUNICATE

9.10 tsamma3o w 7iTTo X bi l3amuud lmaZbuuT:

	a	b	c	d	e	f	g
Sa7							
ghalaT							

9.11 ghayyro[change] lkalimeet[words] yalle[which] |b khaTT ghaami2[bold type]:

| shu ra7 ta3mul **l2usbuu3 ljeey**?   (mish/ma) ra7 **shuuf film 7ilo.** |

9.12 tbeedalo: Find out what a couple of other (real or imaginary) individuals are doing this week(end).

9.13 Prepare a **sketch** with a: beginning   (greetings/scene setting)
middle   (problem)   eg The person asked changes their mind several times about what they are going to do.
end   (resolution)   eg They are finally sure (eg halla2 Sirt mit2akkid *Now I am sure*).

9.14 t7addaso (tzakkaro l2as2ile w l2ajwibe):
1 greetings 2 feeling 3 nationality 4 address | phone no.
5 occupation 6 family 7 cafe 8 past activities 9 **future activities**

UNIT 10
When shall we meet?

1 greetings | name **2** feeling **3** nationality **4** address | phone no. **5** occupation **6** family **7** cafe **8** past activities **9** future activities **10** time | date | doing now **11** places | transport | directions **12** hotel **13** restaurant **14** shopping **15** pastimes | taste **16** tourism | weather

 samiir w layla

1 S (3a ttalifoon) shu layla? hayi2tik[seem] mashghuule[busy] ktiir bi ha l2iyyeem[days].
2 L 2e, samiir, 2imme ba3da mariiDa[sick] w 3am bishtighil ktiir.
3 S Tayyib, 2ayya[which] see3a[hour] btikhlaSe[finish] shshighl[work] lyoom?
4 L bikhlaS mit2akhkhra[late], ssee3a[o'clock] sab3a lmasa[evening]. |2addeesh ssee3a|[what's the time] halla2?
5 S ssee3a khamse. ya3ne[that means] ma fiina nitlee2a[meet] lyoom?
6 L la2, lyoom ra7 ykuun Sa3b[difficult] ktiir. gheer[another] nhaar 2iza[if] baddak.
7 S Tayyib, 2imtiin[when] fiina nitlee2a[meet], lakeen[then]?
8 L |b2addeesh shshahr|[what's the date] lyoom?
9 S leesh, Saar[it has come to] leezim[having to] |neekhud maw3id|[make an appointment] ma3ik 2abl[prior] b[by] shahr[month] ta[to] nshuufik bi ha l2iyyeem?
10 L bala[without] maSkhara[mocking] samiir. 3am bis2al[I'm asking] li2anno[because] |bi 3ashra shshahr|[on the tenth of the month], 2imme 3inda[has] maw3id ma3 l7akiim[doctor].
11 S fi[there is] ba3d[still] tleet tiyyeem[days] 2abl 3ashra shshahr. 2ayya nhaar ra7 ykuun 3indik wa2t[time]?
12 L Tayyib, shu bineesbak[suits], bukra[tomorrow] 2aw[or] |ba3d bukra|[the day after tomorrow]?
13 S bukra Tab3an.
14 L lakeen khalliina[let's] nitlee2a bi nafs[same] l2ahwe, ssee3a sitte w rib3[quarter] lmasa.
15 S bkhaaTrik, layla. bshuufik huniik[there].

1 (On the phone) What['s happening] Layla? You seem very busy these days.
2 Yes, Samir, Mum is still ill. And I'm working a lot.
3 Ok, what time do you finish work today?
4 I finish late, at 7 pm. What's the time now?
5 It's 5 o'clock. Does that mean that we can't meet today?
6 No, today will be very difficult. Another day if you want.
7 Fine, when can we meet then?
8 What's the date today?
9 Why, has it come to having to make an appointment a month in advance to see you these days?
10 Stop mocking, Samiir. I'm asking because on the tenth, Mum has an appointment with the doctor.
11 There are still three days before the tenth. What day will you have time?
12 Ok, what suits you, tomorrow or the day after?
13 Tomorrow, of course.
14 In that case, let's meet at the same cafe, at a quarter past six in the evening.
15 Bye, Layla. See you there.

 10.1

1 leesh samiir w layla ma fiyun yitlee2o lyoom?
2 2ayya see3a btikhlaS layla shshighil?
3 2imtiin maw3id 2imma ma3 l7akiim?
4 b2addeesh shshahr keen lamma[when] 7ikyo[spoke] 3a ttalifoon?
5 baddo yitlee2a ma3a ba3d bukra?
6 2ayya see3a ra7 yitlee2o?

UNIT 10

CULTURE

PACE OF LIFE

The Lebanese enjoy a leisurely lifestyle and pace. It, therefore, is not uncommon for them to arrive late at an invitation, party, or concert. Besides enjoying making a grand entrance, they do not feel the pressure of the stressful pace of a heavily industrialised country, as Lebanon relies greatly on holidaying and historical tourism for revenue.

Arab countries may use the Hijri calendar (beginning with Mohammed's emigration to Medina in 622 CE (Start of the Hijri Calendar)) in their internal communications, and the Gregorian calendar (AD) with the rest of the world. The Islamic lunar calendar has 354 days. The year 2000 AD (Anno Domini) corresponds to the Islamic year 1420 AH (Anno Hegirae). The Gregorian calendar is predominantly used in Lebanon.

VOCABULARY

THE TIME lwa2t

What's the time, please?	2addeesh ssee3a, min faDlak?
It's seven o'clock	ssee3a sab3a
It's | five | to/past | seven	ssee3a sab3a | 2illa / w | khamse
ten	3ashra
a quarter	rib3
twenty	tilt
half past	w niSS
twenty-five past	w niSS 2illa khamse
thirty-five past	w niSS w khamse
AM SSib7 PM: in the afternoon ba3d DDohr in the evening lmasa at night bi lleel	

 10.2 Ask & answer: eg 3.55 pm > 2addeesh ssee3a? > ssee3a **2arb3a 2illa khamse (ba3d DDohr).**
1 11.15 am   2 2.20 pm (... tinteen w...) 3 3.25 pm   4 6.40 pm   5 11.45 pm   6 5.55 am

THE DATE tteriikh

THE DAYS l2iyyeem (yoom sg)		THE MONTHS 2ashhor (sg shahr)	
Sunday	l2a7ad	January	kenuun tteene
Monday	ttaneen	February	shbaaT
		March	2adaar
Tuesday	ttaleeta	April	niseen
		May	2ayyaar
Wednesday	l2irb3a	June	7zayraan
		July	tammuuz
Thursday	lkhamiis	August	2aab
		September	2ayluul
Friday	ljim3a	October	tishriin l2awwal
		November	tishriin tteene
Saturday	ssabt	December	kenuun l2awwal

NOTE 10.3 yoom 2iyyeem 24 hour day = **nhaar** aat 12 hour daytime + **leel** layeele 12 hour nighttime

 10.3 Ask & answer: eg Sunday > lyoom shu?   lyoom **l2a7ad**.
1 Friday 2 Monday 3 Thursday 4 Saturday 5 Wednesday 6 Tuesday

 10.4 Ask & answer: eg 25 July 2002 >
b2addeesh shshahr lyoom? lyoom bi |**khamsaw 3ishriin** | **tammuuz** | **2alfeen w tneen**.
1 09 April 2000 **2** 01 September 2012 **3** 30 January 2010 **4** 23 October 2005 **5** 13 May 1915 **6** 25 December 2013

UNIT 10

 10.5 Give genuine answers: 1 2ayya see3a bit2uum/e^(get up) 3aadatan^(usually) SSib7? b2uum ssee3a...
2 2ayya see3a btuuSal/e^(arrive) 3aadatan 3a shshighil / lmadrase?
3 2ayya see3a btirja3/e^(return) 3aadatan 3a lbeet mni shshighil / lmadrase?
4 shu hinne 2iyyeem niheeyit l2usbuu3?
5 bi 2ayya shahr / 2ashhor 3iTlit^(holiday) ssine^(year)? bi...
6 2imtiin^(when) |3iid mileed**ak**|^(birthday)? bi...

THE SEASONS lifSuul			
winter shshite Dec. Jan. Feb.	**spring** rrabii3 Mar. Apr. May.	**summer** SSeef Jun. Jul. Aug.	**autumn** lkhariif Sep. Oct. Nov.
kenuun l2awwal	2adaar	7zayraan	2ayluul
kenuun tteene	niseen	tammuuz	tishriin l2awwal
shbaaT	2ayyar	2aab	tishriin tteene

10.6 Ask & answer: shshite >
eg shu hinne 2ashhor shshite bi libneen? **kenuun l2awwal, kenuun tteene w shbaaT**.
1 SSeef   2 rrabii3   3 shshite   4 lkhariif

10.7 Ask & answer: eg 2ayluul > ni7na bi 2ayya **faSl**? ni7na **bi (faSl) lkhariif**
1 tammuuz   2 kenuun tteene   3 2adaar   4 tishriin l2awwal   5 niseen   6 2ayluul

10.8 Ask & answer: eg bi 2ayya faSl mneekhud 3iTlit^(holiday) ssine^(year)? > bi faSl SSeef.
1 mnitzallaj^(ski) 3a ttalj^(snow)?   3 btuu2a3^(fall) wraa2^(leaves) shshajar^(trees)?   5 mnismarr^(tan) bi shshams^(sun)?
2 mnisba7 bi lba7r^(sea)?   4 biwarrdo^(flower) lizhuur^(flowers)?   6 minwalli3^(turn on) ddiffeeye^(heater)?

WHEN 2imtiin?	
three years ago	mni tleet sniin
the year before last	ssine 2abl (ssine) lmaaDye
last year	ssine lmaaDye
last month	shshahr lmaaDe
the day before yesterday	2awwilt mbeeri7
yesterday	mbeeri7
today	lyoom
tomorrow	bukra
the day after tomorrow	ba3d bukra
next month	shshahr ljeey
in three years	ba3d tleet sniin

 10.9 2imtiin lmaw3id^(appointment)? (*2 changes to t when linking eg 2iyyem^(days) but tleet ~~2~~tiyyeem)
eg In three days,   on Friday,   20 August,   at 3.30 pm
   ba3d tleet tiyyeem,   nhaar ljim3a,   bi 3ishriin 2aab,   ssee3a tleete w niSS ba3d DDohr

1 Three days ago,   on Monday,   3 January,   at 5.05 am
2 The day after tomorrow,   on Sunday,   13 May,   at 3.40 pm
3 Yesterday,   on Thursday, 21 October,   at 7.15 pm

10.10 Ask: eg yesterday > b2addeesh shshahr **keen** mbeeri7? (Choose from: bi / keen / ra7 ykuun)
1 lyoom   2 bukra   3 2awwilt mbeeri7   4 ba3d bukra   5 ttaneen lmaaDe   6 l2a7ad ljeey

 10.11 Give the real date: eg b2addeesh shshahr keen mbeeri7? > mbeeri7 **keen bi** ....
(Choose from: bi.../ keen bi....../ra7 ykuun bi.......)
1 b2addeesh shshahr keen ttaleeta lmaaDye?   4 b2addeesh shshahr ra7 ykuun ssabt ljeey?
2 b2addeesh shshahr ra7 ykuun bukra?   5 b2addeesh shshahr keen mbeeri7?
3 b2addeesh shshahr lyoom?   6 b2addeesh shshahr ra7 ykuun ba3d bukra?

UNIT 10

 10.12   CROSSWORD kalimeet mit2aaT3a

Across

1 faSl fi shoob[hot] ktiir.
6 ba3d ttaneen.
9 2awwal[first] shahr bi ssine[year].
11 tna3shar see3it 3atm[darkness].
12 shahr biballish[starts] faSl rrabii3 bi libneen.

Down

2 kill[every] tleet 2ashhor.
3 lfaSl yalle mnitzallaj[ski] fii[in] 3a ttalj[snow].
4 mbeeri7, lyoom, bukra, ...
5 2awwal nhaar ba3d niheeyit l2usbuu3.
7 shahreen ba3d tammuuz.
8 nhaar 2abl ba3d bukra.
10 tna3shar see3it Daww[light].

GRAMMAR

PRESENT CONTINUOUS
am doing

RULE 10.13   To say what is happening now, in English, we use **ing**, in Arabic we use **3am**

eg I am eat**ing**   **3am** beekul

So, you place **3am** before any present verb.

If you end up with a threeeconsonant cluster, drop the b/m of the verb prefix.

eg 3am beekul, but 3am ~~b~~yeekul, 3am bil3ab, but 3am ~~m~~nil3ab

To form the **negative** use: **ma/mish** eg ma/mish 3am beekul, ma/mish 3am neekul

 10.13 Ask: eg bitfarraj 3a ttalfizyoon > shu **3am ta3mul**?

1 byit3allamo[learn] 3arabe   4 byi7ke[speak] 3arabe
2 [m]bi2ra[read] kteeb[book] 7ilo[interesting]   5 [m]bitsamma3 3a[listen to] lim3allim
3 [f]btiktub[write] bi l3arabe   6 [m]nitTalla3 bi[look at] lloo7[board]

 10.14 Answer: eg shu 3am ta3mul? (bitfarraj 3a ttalfizyoon) > **3am bitfarraj 3a ttalfizyoon.**

1 shu 3am ta3mul? (eating a saandwich)   3 shu 3am ta3imlo? (reading a book)   5 shu 3am ya3mul? (doing homework)
2 shu 3am ta3imle? (drinking juice)   4 shu 3am na3mul? (learning Arabic)   6 shu 3am ta3mul[f]? (writing in Arabic)

UNIT 10

 10.15 Give a genuine answer: shu 3am ta3imlo w shu mish/ma 3am ta3imlo halla2^{now}?
  eg bit3allam^{learn} 3arabe > **3am bit3allam 3arabe** ‖ bil3ab faTbool > **ma/mish 3am bil3ab faTbool**.
  1 beekul saandwish jibne.
  2 bitnaffas^{breathing} hawa^{air}.
  3 bishrab biira.
  4 bit3allam 3arabe.
  5 bitfarraj 3a ttalfizyoon.
  6 bi7ke w biktub bi l3arabe.

COMPREHEND & COMMUNICATE

 10.16 tsamma3o w 7iTTo X bi l3amuud lmaZbuuT:

	Sa7	ghalaT
a		
b		
c		
d		
e		
f		

 10.17 ghayyro lkalimeet yalle b khaTT ghaami2:

2as2ile	2ajwibe
2addeesh ssee3a?	ssee3a **khamse w tilt**.
lyoom shu?	lyoom **l2irb3a**.
b2addeesh shshahr **lyoom**?	lyoom bi **khamsaw 3ishriin, niseen, 2alfeen w 3ashra**.
ni7na bi2ayya **faSl**?	ni7na bi faSl **lkhariif**.
2imtiin 3iid mileed**ak**?	3iid milleede bi **tleete 7zayraan, 2alf w tisi3 miyye w tmeenaw sittiin**.

 10.18 tbeedalo with a couple of other (real or imaginary) individuals:
  the time, day, date, season, birthday, and current activity.

10.19 7aDDro^{prepare} **sketsh** fiya^{in it} lwa2t w tteriikh w: bideeye^{beginning} w mishikle^{problem} w 7all^{resolution}
(lmishikle, masalan^{eg}, the person tells you the wrong time or date, or you can't agree on an appointment date.)

 10.20 t7addaso (tzakkaro l2as2ile w l2ajwibe):
  1 greetings 2 feeling 3 nationality 4 address | phone no. 5 occupation 6 family 7 cafe
  8 past activities 9 future activities 10 time | date | activity now

UNIT 11
Where is the station?

DIALOGUE

1 greetings | name   2 feeling   3 nationality   4 address | phone no.   5 occupation   6 family   7 cafe   8 past activities   9 future activities
10 time | date | doing now   **11 places | transport | directions**   12 hotel   13 restaurant   14 shopping   15 pastimes | taste   16 tourism | weather

 samiir w layla

1 S (3a ttalifoon) shukran layla 3a l3aziime^{invitation}. 2akhiiran^{finally}! 2e, Tab3an b7ibb 2ije. bas ween baytkun |bi ZZabT|^{exactly}?
2 L khood lbooSTa^{bus} ra2im 3ashra min see7it^{square} lma3raD^{exhibition} w nzaal$^{get\ off}$ khams m7aTTaat^{stops} ba3d ljeem3a.
3 S ya3ne^{means} ma fi laff^{turning} 3a lyamiin^{right} 2aw lyasaar^{left}? bas^{when} 2inzal min lbooSTa bruu7 jeelis^{straight} 7atta^{till} 2uuSal^{arrive} 3a baytkun?
4 L bas tinzal min lbooSTa, 2Taa3^{cross} shsheeri3 w mshii^{walk} Soob^{towards} lfarmashiyye^{chemist}. baytna 2abl^{before} lmadrase bi shwayy.
5 S mish 3am saddi2^{believe}! 3idiile^{repeat}, 2imtiin bije?
6 L samiir hayde teelit marra^{time} b3idlak^{repeat}, yoom ssabt ljeey sse3a tleete w niSS.
7 S 3miltiine ktiir mabSuuT. shukran ktiir, layla. kint 3am bitsee2al^{wondering} 2imtiin ra7 yije ha nnhar^{day} l7ilo.
8 L 2ana kameen ra7 kuun mabSuTa.
9 S miin ra7 ykuun bi lbeet?
10 L ra7 tit3arraf^{meet} 3a l3ayle killa. lmaama w lbaaba w kill 2ikhiwte ra7 ykuuno bi lbeet.
11 S shu ra2yik^{opinion}, ra7 y7ibbuune?
12 L |law ma|$^{even\ if\ not}$ 7abbuuk ra7 ykuuno luTafa ma3ak. ma tkhaaf$^{be\ afraid}$!
13 S nshalla!
14 L bas ma tinsa^{forget} tilbus^{wear} ta2m^{suit} w tlammi3^{polish} SibbaaTak^{shoes}. 2imme naZara^{vision} ktiir 2awe^{strong}.
15 S ma tkhaafe; ma ra7 2ije 3a lbisikleet w bi lbroteel^{singlet}. bshuufik ssabt.

1 (On the phone) Thank you, Layla, for the invite. Finally! Yes, of course, I'd like to come. But where exactly is your house?
2 Catch bus no. 10 from see7it lma3raD Square and get off five stops after the university.
3 Does that mean there's no turning right or left? When I get off the bus, I go straight till I get to your house?
4 When you get off the bus, cross the street and walk towards the pharmacy. Our house is just before the school.
5 I can't believe it! Tell me again, when do I come?
6 Samir, that's the third time I repeat, next Saturday at half past three.
7 You've made me very happy. Thank you so much, Layla. I was wondering when this beautiful day would come.
8 Also I will be happy.
9 Who will be at home?
10 You're going to meet the whole family. Mum, Dad and all my siblings will be at home.
11 What do you think; will they like me?
12 Even if they don't like you, they will be nice to you. Don't worry!
13 I hope so!
14 But don't forget to wear a suit and polish your shoes. My mother's vision is very sharp.
15 Don't worry; I won't come on a bike, wearing a singlet. See you Saturday.

 11.1

1 2imtiin ma3zuum^{invited} samiir |3ind layla|$^{at\ Layla's}$?
2 shu byeekhud samiir ta^{to} yruu7 la 3ind layla?
3 beet layla 2abl 2aw^{or} ba3d lmadrase?
4 3a miin ra7 yit3arraf samiir?
5 ra7 ykuun bayy layla bi lbeet kameen?
6 leesh leezim samiir ylammi3 SibbaaTo?

UNIT 11

CULTURE

TRANSPORT

The Lebanese can only reminisce with frustration about the 'Thousand and One Nights', when the magic carpet could glide you romantically across a fairyland. On the ground, they face the daily negotiating of peak-hour traffic, exacerbated by the relatively large number of cars per capita.

Very affordable public transport is readily available wherever you are. You can choose to hail a passing cab or jump on a minibus criss-crossing the main cities or between them.

If you are a constant user of public transport, you may have no need to read the thirteen daily newspapers, as, in a shared taxi or on the bus, people may readily exchange information and opinions, and even vent to a sympathetic ear.

VOCABULARY

PLACES 2ameekin

hospital	mistashfa^{yeet}
train / bus station	m7aTTit ttreen / lbaaS
train / bus stop	maw2if ttreen / lbaaS
police station	makhfar^{makhaafir} shshirTa
airport	maTaar^{aat}
school	madrase^{madeeris}
university	jeem3a^{at}
market	suu2^{2aswee2}
bookshop	maktabe^{et}

11.2 Ask for directions: eg badde 2ishitre tyeeb^{clothes}. > la^{to} ween^{where} **bruu7** ta^{to} 2ishitre tyeeb?

1 baddo yit3allam 3arabe.
2 baddun yishitro kteeb.
3 2immun mariiDa.
4 nsara2na$^{were\ robbed}$.
5 baddak tseefir bi ttreen.
6 badda teekhud TTiyyaara^{plane}.

11.3 Tell those in the above exercise where to go: eg badde^m 2ishitre tyeeb. > ruu7$^{e\backslash o}$ 3a **ssuu2**

MEANS OF TRANSPORT   wasee2il nna2l

by bus	**bi** l2otobiis / lbooSTa / lbaaS
car	ssiyyaara / siyyaarte
taxi	ttaksi
train	ttreen
plane	TTiyyaara
boat	lmarkab
bicycle	**3a** lbisikleet
motorbike	lmotorsiikl
on foot	mashe

11.4 Ask for directions: eg 2ana | 3a ssuu2 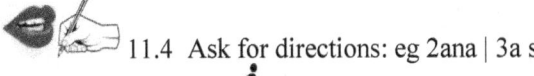 > kiif **bruu7** 3a ssuu2?

1 hiyye | 3a lmadrase
2 hinne | 3a lmistashfa
3 2into | 3a ljeem3a
4 huwwe | 3a lmaTaar
5 ni7na | 3a libraziil
6 2inte | 3a ssuu2

11.5 Tell those in the above exercise what means to use: eg 2ana | 3a ssuu2  > ruu7$^{e\backslash o}$ **bi ttreen**.

UNIT 11

Verb\s fi3l\2af3aal	
walk/go on foot	msh**ii**$^{i\backslash u}$ / ruu7$^{e\backslash o}$ mashe
go right	ruu7$^{e\backslash o}$ 3a lyamiin
turn (take the) left	liff$^{e\backslash o}$ 3a lyasaar/lishmeel
cross the street	2T**aa**3$^{a3e\backslash a3o}$ TTarii2
catch the bus	kh**ood**$^{ide\backslash ido}$ lbooSTa / lbaaS
get off at the school	nz**aal**$^{ale\backslash alo}$ 3ind lmadrase

 11.6 Tell them how to get there: eg kiif bruu7^m 3a ssuu2? > **khood ttreen.**

1 kiif bruu7^m 3a lmadrase? 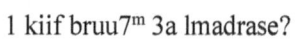   3 kiif minruu7 3a ljeem3a? ←   5 kiif minruu7 3a ljeem3a? 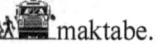maktabe.

2 kiif bruu7^f 3a lmistashfa 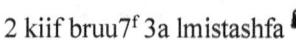   4 kiif bruu7^m 3a lmaTaar? →   6 kiif bruu7^f 3a ssuu2? cross

Preposition 7arf jar	
next to	7add
in front of | behind	2iddeem | wara
before | after	2abl | ba3d

 11.7 Say where the place is: eg ween ssuu2? (next to) m7aTTit ttreen > **7add** m7aTTit ttreen.

1 ween lmistashfa? (in front of) m7aTTit lbaaS.   4 ween bayta? (next to) lmistashfa.
2 ween lmadrase? (behind) lmaTaar.   5 ween ljeem3a? (after) makhfar shshirTa.
3 ween lmaktabe? (before) m7aTTit ttreen.   6 ween shighlik? (across from/in front of) ssuu2

Adverb Zarf	
to the right	3a lyamiin
to the left	lyasaar / shshmeel
straight ahead	jeelis / dighre

11.8 Give directions: kiif **bruu7**^{f} 3a lmistashfa?

Turn ← Catch  No.10. Get off  Go by  to^{la}    HOSPITAL

 11.9 Ask: eg I come > **kiif bije?**$^{how\ do\ I\ come?}$

bije^{come} / jiit^{came}		
2ana bije^{jiit}	2inta btije^{jiit}	huwwe byije^{2ija}
ni7na mnije^{jiina}	2inte btije^{jiite}	hiyye btije^{2ijit}
	2into btijo^{jiito}	hinne byijo^{2ijo}

1 They come 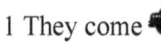 2 You^p come 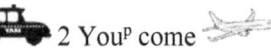 3 She comes 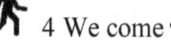 4 We come  5 You^f come  6 He comes

 11.10 Tell those in the above exercise how to come: eg Come by > ta3**a**$^{e\backslash o}$ bi lmarkab

UNIT 11

GRAMMAR

PAST (was doing) & FUTURE (am going to/will be doing) CONTINUOUS TENSES

11.11 Complete the table: (Revise the verb *to be* before proceeding: bkuun (see 7.7) and kint (see 8.3).

	Present continuous (**am doing**)	Past continuous (**was doing**)	Future continuous (**am going to\will be doing**)	
2ana	*I am eating* **3am** beekul	*I was eating* **kint 3am** beekul	*I am going to be* **ra7 kuun 3am** beekul	*I will be eating* **bkuun 3am** beekul
ni7na	**3am** neekul	**kinna 3am** neekul	**ra7 nkuun 3am** neekul	**minkuun 3am** neekul
2inta	**3am** teekul	**kint 3am** teekul	**ra7 tkuun 3am** teekul	**bitkuun 3am** teekul
⋮	⋮	⋮	⋮	⋮

11.12 Ask: eg ssee3a khamse (I^m was learning) Arabic. > shu **kint 3am ta3mul** ssee3a khamse?
1 ssee3a tleete (she was doing) farDa.   4 ssee3a sitte (he was swimming).
2 ssee3a tis3a (we will be drinking).   5 ssee3a tna3sh (you^p were playing) tenis.
3 ssee3a sab3a (you^m are going to be eating).   6 ssee3a tinteen (they are going to be working).

11.13 What are the answers to the questions in the above exercise?
eg ssee3a khamse, I was learning Arabic. > ssee3a khamse **kint 3am bit3allam 3arabe**.

OBJECT PRONOUNS
me, us | you^m you^f you^p him, her, them

11.14 Follow the rule to complete the table:

RULE 11.14
- To add a pronominal suffix to a verb ending in a **consonant**: add, the usual eg ^he brought jeeb^ne\na | ak\ik\kun | o\a\un
- To add a pronominal suffix to a verb ending in a **vowel**:

  1. Change the vowel to the following long vowels:

	except for '**hiyye** and '**hinne** where:
a becomes **ee** (**aa**^if guttural)	**a** becomes **aah**
o becomes **uu**	**o** becomes **uw**
e becomes **ii**	**e** becomes **iy**

  2. Start the suffix with a consonant^see table below

		Verb ends in a:					
Consonant		Vowel					
		a		o		e	
jeeb	lee2a	khabba	7abbo	sa2alo	bta3Te	bitna22e	
he brought	*he met*	*he hid*	*they liked*	*they asked*	*you give*	*she chooses*	
	ne^me		khabb**ee**|ne	7abb**uu**|ne	sa2al**uu**|ne	bta3T**ii**|ne	bitna22**ii**|ne
	na^us	ne^me	...	...	...	...	...
	ak^you m	na^us	...	...	...	...	...
jeeb	ik^you f	k^you m	...	...	...	...	...
	kun^you p	le2aa	ke^you f	...	...	...	...	...
		kun^you p	...	...	...	...	...
	o^him	him	...	...	...	...	...
	a^her	ha^her	...	7abb**uw**a	...	bta3T**iy**a	...
	un^them	hun^them	...	**uw**un	...	**iy**yun	...

UNIT 11

 11.15 eg lee2a (them) bi l2ahwe > le2aahun bi l2ahwe.
1 jeeb (you^f) 3a^to lmadrase. 3 khabba (them) wara lbeeb. 5 sa2alo (him) su2aal.
2 lee2a (us) bi lim7aTTa. 4 7abbo (her) li2anna keenit laTiife. 6 ^hiyye bta3Te (you^m) maSaare^money.

 11.16 What questions can be asked in the above exercise:
eg lee2a (them) bi l2ahwe. > ween^where le2aahun? (Use: (la^to) ween^where? shu? leesh^why?)

COMPREHEND & COMMUNICATE

 11.17 tsamma3o w 7iTTo X bi l3amuud lmaZbuuT.

	a	b	c	d	e	f	g	h	i	j
Sa7										
ghalaT										

 11.18 ghayyro lkalimeet yalle bi khaTT ghaami2

2as2ile	2ajwibe
la ween **bruu7** ta 2ishitre tyeeb?	**ruu7** 3a **ssuu2**.
kiif **bruu7** 3a **ssuu2**, 3mool ma3ruuf?	khood lbaaS ra2m **5**, w **nzaal** 3ind lmadrase. khood **2awwal** sheeri3 3a **lyamiin** w ba3deen^then **liff 3a lyasaar**.
ween **ssuu2**, min faDlak?	ruu7 jeelis 7atta **tuuSal** 3a lmistashfa. ssuu2 bikuun **wara** ljeemi3.
kiif **bije**?	ta3a bi lmarkab.
ween **ble2iik**^e\kun?	le2iine bi l2ahwe.

 11.19 tbeedalo with a couple of other (real or imaginary) individuals:
1 how they get to school/work.
2 directions to the town/city centre, from where they are: (a) by public transport (b) on foot.

 11.20 7aDDro^prepare **sketsh** fiya^in it ti3limeet w bideeye^beginning w mishikle^problem w 7all^resolution.

 11.21 t7addaso^Converse (tzakkaro l2as2ile w l2ajwibe)
1 greetings **2** feeling **3** nationality **4** address | phone no. **5** occupation **6** family **7** cafe **8** past activities
9 future activities **10** time | date | am doing **11** places | transport | directions | was//going to/will be doing

UNIT 12
Do you have a room for two?

DIALOGUE

1 greetings | name 2 feeling 3 nationality 4 address | phone no. 5 occupation 6 family 7 cafe 8 past activities 9 future activities
10 time | date | activity now 11 places | transport | directions 12 **hotel** 13 restaurant 14 shopping 15 pastimes | taste 16 tourism | weather

   samiir w layla

1 S mish 3am saddi2 2inno 3ayiltik 7abbitne w baddun yshufuune 2aktar^more! biTlublik^order 2ahwe teenye^another?
2 L khiliS wa2t lghada^lunch. leezim 2irja3 3a shshighil. w 2ana ktiir mirtee7a^relieved 2inno 3ajabun^liked ta2mak.
3 S ra7 ykuun Sa3b^difficult ma shuufik la tleet tiyyem, layla. |ntibhe 3a|look after 7aalik^yourself.
4 L ruu7 w rja3le bi ssaleeme. bkhaaTrak, samiir. 2alla ma3ak. ra7 ruu7 2abilma^before tdammi3^tear 3ayne^eye.
   (samiir 3a ttalifoon ma3 Saa7ib^owner l2oteel (S2)
5 S mar7aba. hayda 2oteel Traablus^Tripoli?
6 S2 na3am. kiif fiine 2ikhidmak^serve?
7 S ra7 2ije^come b shighil 3a Traablus. 3indkun ma7all^vacancy?
8 S2 la kam shakhS?
9 S la shakhS waa7ad.
10 S2 na3am, fi *3inna^have ghirfe^room la shakhS waa7ad. fiya takht^bed la waa7ad.
11 S bas min faDlak, badde ykuun ttakht 2akbar^bigger. 2iza bikuun la tneen bikuun murii7^comfortable 2aktar. w badde ykuun fi bi lghirfe 7immeem^bathroom ma3 baanyo^bath w duush^shower. w ykuun fiya kameen shibbeek^window w balkoon w l2internet, Tab3an.
12 S2 ma fi mishikle. ra7 na3Tiik 2a7san^best ghirfe 3inna w ma3a manZar^view kameen, bas ra7 tkallfak^cost 2aktar shwayy.
13 S ya3ne^meaning/so b2addeesh hiyye?
14 S2 hayde lghirfe bi tmeniin dolar bi lyoom.
15 S mish mishikle li2anno shshirke^company ra7 tidfa3. 7jizle^book yyeeha^it w bshuufkun bukra lakeen. bkhaaTrak.
   *short for 3indna

1 I can't believe that your family liked me and wants to see more of me! Should I order you another coffee?
2 Lunchtime is over. I have to go back to work. Also I am very relieved that they liked your suit.
3 It's going to be hard not seeing you for three days, Layla. Take care of yourself.
4 Go and come back to me safely. Bye, Samir. God be with you. I'll go before I get teary eyed.
   (Samir on the phone with the hotel owner)
5 Hello. Is this Tripoli Hotel?
6 Yes. How can I be of service to you?
7 I'm coming to Tripoli for work. Do you have room?
8 For how many people?
9 For one person.
10 Yes, we have a room for one person. It has a single bed.
11 But, if you please, I'd like a bigger bed. If it's for two, it'll be more comfortable. And I'd like the room to have a bathroom with a bath and shower; also a window, a balcony and the internet, of course.
12 No problem. We'll give you the best room we have. It also has a view, but it'll cost you a bit more.
13 So how much is it?
14 This room costs eighty dollars a day.
15 Not a problem because the company will pay. Reserve it for me and I'll see you tomorrow then. Bye.

12.1 1 la kam yoom mseefir samiir?   4 leesh bifaDDil takht kbiir?
      2 la kam shakhS byi7juz?   5 b2addeesh lghirfe?
      3 shu noo3^type ttakht yalle^which baddo yyee? 6 leesh ghaalye^expensive?

UNIT 12

CULTURE

HOTEL ACCOMMODATION

Lebanon is a favoured tourist destination for the Lebanese living abroad. Visitors from the gulf escaping the heat of desert climates compete with them in the summer for sea chalets, and cool sea and mountain resorts. This means that those who wish to go there in the warmer seasons need to book well in advance to secure quickly booked out hotel accommodation.

Hotels thrive when seaagoers, gourmet food seekers and night-reveller myriads grace Lebanon's shores. The hotel industry is, therefore, a crucial service provider and plays a vital role in the Lebanese economy.

VOCABULARY

HOTEL 2oteel

Type of room	noo3 lghirfe
room for two / three	ghirfe la shakhSeen / tleet 2ashkhaaS
single / double bed	takht[tkhuute] zghiir / kbiir
with breakfast	ma3 ttirwii2a
bathroom	7immeem
bath	baanyo
shower	duush
soap	Sabuune
towel	manshafe[maneeshif]
balcony	balkoon[blekiin]
window	shibbeek[shbebiik]
internet	2internet
room service	khidmit lghiraf
for one / two night(s)	la layle / layilteen / tleet layeele
view	manZar[manaaZir]

 12.2 eg: 3indak ghirfe .... , 2iza bitriid?

eg	1	2	3	4	5	6
la **tleet layeele**?	1 night	4 nights	7 nights	3 nights	2 nights	2 weeks
la **shakhSeen**?	1 person	3 people	5 people	2 people	4 people	1 person
fiya **takht kbiir**	double bed	3 single beds	1 double+3 single	2 single beds	4 single beds	double bed
w **7immeem**	bathroom+shower	balcony+view	phone	2internet+breafast	bathroom+bath	large balcony

UNIT 12

12.3 Pick the appropriate question from the following: eg la tleet 2ashkhaaS > **la kam shakhS?**
   la kam layle?   la kam shakhS?   kam takht?   shu bit7ibb^{elo} ykuun fi bi lghirfe?
1 badde ykuun fiya takhteen.   3 badde ykuun fiya 7immemeen.   5 badde ykuun fiya balkoon.
2 la shakhS waa7ad.   4 la 2arba3 layeele.   6 la sitt 2ashkhaaS.

Verbs	2af3aal
to stay in a hotel	binzal^{nzilt} bi 2oteel
to stay for two days	bib2a^{b2iit} yomeen
to book	bi7juz^{7ajazt}
to leave the key	bitruk^{tarakt} lmiftee7
to go on a tour	bruu7^{ri7t} ra7le^{et}
to wake up for breakfast	bfii2^{fi2t} 3a ttirwii2a
to take up one's luggage	bTalli3^{Talla3t} shshanta^{shshinat}

12.4 Number the following actions according to the order you did them during your last summer holidays:
a 7ajazt w seefart 3a lQaahira^{Cairo}.   d nzilt bi 2oteel la tmeen tiyyeem^{days}.
b tarakt l2oteel ta zuur lmat7af.   e fi2t w nzilt 3a ttirwii2a.
c tarakt miftee7 lghirfe ma3 *|maktab l2isti2beel|. f see3adne mwaZZaf l2oteel ta Talli3 shshanta.
   * reception desk

GRAMMAR

COMPARISON ttifDiil

RULE 12.5 For the **comparative**$^{comparing\ two\ things}$:
• strip the adjective of all its vowels down to its three consonant root.
• place **2a** at its beginning and **a** after the second consonant: eg kbiir > kbr > **2akbar**^{bigger}
For the **superlative**$^{comparing\ more\ than\ two\ things}$: comparative + **shi**   eg   2akbar shi^{biggest}

 12.5 Fill in the table:

adjective	comparative (more than)	superlative (the most)
Tawiil^{tall} / 2aSiir^{short}	2aTwal (min^{than}) / 2a2Sar (min)	2aTwal shi / 2a2Sar shi
naaSi7^{fat} / D3iif^{skinny}	...	...
laTiif / la2iim	...	...

12.6 Using **is,** draw the following comparisons eg Samir **is** nice:
1 samiir laTiif^{nice} bas layla **2alTaf**. layla 2alTaf minno w min tom. hiyye 2alTaf minnun. layla **2alTaf shi**.
2 samiir 7ilo ...
3 samiir ghane^{rich} ...

 12.7 Read the note and ask for what you want: eg **a** bigger room   >   badde **ghirfe 2akbar**, 3mool ma3ruuf.
                                                           the biggest room> badde **2akbar ghirfe**, 3mool ma3ruuf.

NOTE 12.7 With **a/the,** you can shift the **position** of the adjective for a comparative or superlative result:
The **comparative** can be expressed by placing the comparative form **after** the noun   eg ghirfe 2akbar *a bigger room*.
The **superlative** can be expressed by placing the comparative form **before** the noun eg 2akbar ghirfe *the biggest room*.
   1 a larger bed.   3 a more beautiful view.   5 the cheapest^{rkhiiS} room |you have|^{3indak}.
   2 faster^{sarii3} internet.   4 the largest balcony.   6 the widest^{3ariiD} bath you^{f} have.

UNIT 12

OBJECT PRONOUNS

NOTE 12.8
A verb cannot have two suffixes appended to it. The personal suffix is attached to the verb, while the **object pronoun** follows separately after. So, in a sentence like:
- Book it (the room) for me *7jizle yyeeha'*, **le**[for me] is suffixed to the verb, and **yyeeha**[it] follows separately.
- The separate object pronouns (it[mf]/them) take the following forms: yyee[m]   yyeeha[f]   yyeehun[p]

 12.8 Match the words in the three columns (the separate object *pronoun is in bold type)*:

1 Give **them** to him	a 3Tii	a **yyee**
2 Give **it**[f] to me	b 3Tiina	b **yyeeha**
3 Give **it**[m] to us	c 3Tiine	c **yyeehun**

 12.9 Ask &answer: eg hinne fata7uule lbeeb > shu 3**imlo**? fata7uule **yyee**
1 layla 3aTitkun l2alam.
2 2ikhte 7ajazitle lghirfe.
3 Sadii2o shtaraalo[buy] lkutub.
4 lkhaadim[servant] Talla3la lmiftee7.
5 samiir 2akhadla zzhuur[flowers].
6 2into fata7tuulun shibbeek l7immeem.

COMPREHEND & COMMUNICATE

12.10 tsamma3o w 7iTTo X bi l3amuud lmaZbuuT:

	a	b	c	d	e	f	g	h	i	j
Sa7										
ghalaT										

12.11 ghayyro lkalimeet yalle bi khaTT ghaami2:

> 3indkun ghirfe la **tleet** layeele, la **shakhSeen**, fiya takht **kbiir** w **7immeem**, **2iza bitriid**?

12.12 Book with an imaginary hotel receptionist the sort of room you'd like in Beirut, Lebanon.

12.13 7aDDro **sketsh** 3an 7ajz[booking] bi 2oteel fiya: bideeye, mishikle, w 7all.

12.14 t7addaso (tzakkaro l2as2ile w l2ajwibe):
1 greetings 2 feeling 3 nationality 4 address | phone no. 5 occupation 6 family 7 cafe 8 past activities 9 future activities 10 time | date | am doing 11 places | transport | directions **12 hotel**

UNIT 13
A plate of 7ummuS, please.

DIALOGUE

1 greetings | name   2 feeling   3 nationality   4 address | phone no.   5 occupation   6 family   7 cafe   8 past activities   9 future activities   10 time | date | activity now   11 places | transport | directions   12 hotel   **13 restaurant**   14 shopping   15 pastimes | taste   16 tourism | weather

samiir w layla w lgarsoon[waiter] (W)

1 L leesh ya samiir 3azamitne[invite] lyoom 3a hayda lmaT3am[restaurant]? ktiir ghaale!
2 S lyoom yoom muhimm[important], layla. khalliina[let's] niTlub |2awwal shi|[first thing], w ba3deen[afterwards] ra7 2illik[tell] leesh.
3 L nshalla tkuun lkilfe[cost] bti7ruz[worth it]!
4 S ya m3allim, |liistit l2akl|[menu] w lmashruub, min faDlak.
5 W 7aaDir[sure]. haay[here's] liistit l2akl w haay liistit lmashruub. birja3 ba3d[after] shwayy.
6 S la2, mish Daruure[necessary]. jibilna[bring] 2anniinit 3ara2[Arak] w keeseen[glass] 2awwal shi ma3 lmeeza[entrees]: |kibbe nayye|[raw meat], tabbuule, mtabbal[marinated] batinjeen[eggplant] w 7ummuS. w ba3deen baddna Sa7n[dish] samak[fish] mishwe[grilled] w Sa7n djeej[chicken] 3a[on] rizz[rice], w shisheen[skewers] kafta*, 2iza bitriid.
7 W tikramo[sure].
8 L samiir ra7 ykuun |ktiir 3leek|[too much for you]. fahhimne[explain], leesh jibitna la hoon?
9 S ma fi shi ghaale 3layke[when it comes to you], layla. Sarle[it has been for me] midde[a while] badde 2is2alik su2aal[question] bas khaayif[afraid].
10 L su2aal shu? khaayif min shu? shu 3am bikhawwfak[frighten], samiir? 7kii[speak]. mish 3am bi2dir[able to] 2inTur[wait] ba2a[anymore]. 2ille!
11 S layla, ... 2ana ... badde ... 2illik ... 2inno[that] ... 2inno ....
12 L 2e, samiir, 7kii. 2uul shu .... 2uul .... 7kii ....!
13 W tfaDDalo, haay lkeeseen. nshalla yi3jibkun[to your taste] l3ara2. w haay lmeeza. w ba3d shwayy bjibilkun liS7uun lbee2ye[remaining] yalle Talabtuwa.
14 S layla... ya[either] mnishrab kees khTuubitna, ya[or] b2uum[get up] halla2 w bimshe[leave]!

* A mix of spiced meat and parsley often served on a skewer.

1 Why, Samir, did you invite me today to this restaurant? It's very expensive.
2 Today is an important day, Layla. Let's order first and then I'll tell you why.
3 I hope the cost will be worth it!
4 Waiter, the food and drink menu, please.
5 Sure. Here's the food menu and here's the drink menu. I'll come back in a little while.
6 No, that's not necessary. Bring us a bottle of arak and two glasses for a start with the entrees: the raw meat dish, tabuli, baba ghanuj, and hummus. Then we'll have two plates of grilled fish, chicken on rice, and two kefta skewers, if you please.
7 Sure.
8 Samir, this will be too much for you. Explain to me, why did you bring us here?
9 Nothing is expensive when it comes to you, Layla. It's been a while since I've wanted to ask you a question but have been afraid.
10 What question? What are you afraid of? What is scaring you, Samir? Speak. I can't wait any longer. Tell me!
11 Layla,...I...want to...tell you...that...that....
12 Yes, Samir, speak. Say what......say......speak.....!
13 Here you are. Here are the two glasses. I hope you'll like the arak. And here are the entrees. I'll come back in a little while with the remaining dishes that you asked for.
14 Layla, either we drink to our engagement or I'll get up now and leave!

 13.1

1 ween layla w samiir?
2 leesh layla ma badda hayda lmaT3am?
3 shu byiTlub samiir ka mashruub?
4 shu byiTlub samiir ka meeza?
5 leesh samiir Tawwal[take so long] ta yis2al su2aalo?
6 kees shu baddo yishrab?

UNIT 13

CULTURE

RESTAURANT COURSES

A typical restaurant meal in Lebanon is one that starts with mini appetizer dishes called meeza. A meeza may also just be an accompaniment to arak or whisky drinking at any occasion.

Do not be surprised if one of those meeza dishes is kibbe nayye, finely ground (traditionally in an earthenware urn) raw meat, with crushed wheat and added spices. It has to be served fresh.

A meal usually finishes with Lebanese coffee and a variety of sweets to choose from.

The Lebanese do not wait for a restaurant outing to indulge in a meeza. Such a banquet is frequently enjoyed at a soiree with friends, a Sunday family gathering or any other occasion that calls for conviviality or celebration.

VOCABULARY

RESTAURANT maT3am

ORDERING TTalab

waiter/waitress	(to call them) ya m3allim / ya sitt (to refer to them) lgarsoon
menu	liistit l2akl
entree/appetisers	mu2abbileet / meeza
meal/main meal/snack	wajbe^{eet} / wajbe ra2isiyye / wajbe khafiife
breakfast/lunch/dinner	tirwii2a/ghada/3asha
dessert	7ilo^{7ilweyeet}
plate/dish	Sa7n

 13.2 Ask: eg menu > **liistit l2akl**, 3mool ma3ruuf.

1 appetizers 2 plate of falafel 3 dessert and coffee
4 just a snack 5 tea, no (biduun) sugar *sikkar* 6 coffee, no milk (7aliib).

DRINK^s mashruub^{eet}

a glass of arak	kees 3ara2
wine (white / red)	nbiid (2abyaD / 2a7mar)

 13.3 Answer: eg can of coke > shu btishrab? **tankit koola**, min faDlak.

1 can of Fanta. 2 bottle of beer. 3 glass of white wine.
4 bottle of red wine. 5 glass of arak. 6 glass of orange juice.

DISHE\S Sa7n \ S7uun

meat	la7me
chicken	djeej / farruuj $^{grilled\ takeaway}$
lamb / beef / pork	la7m| kharuuf / ba2ar / khanziir
fish / seafood	samak / ma2kuleet ba7riyye
salad	slaaTa

UNIT 13

 13.4 Answer to order: eg chicken > shu noo3^type lla7me? Sa7n **djeej**, 2iza bitriid.
   1 beef   2 pork   3 fish   4 lamb   5 chicken   6 seafood

COOKING STYLE Tarii2it TTabkh	
cooked / raw	maTbuukh / nayy
boiled	masluu2
grilled	mishwe
fried	mi2le
a stew	yakhne
baked	makhbuuz

 13.5 Order: eg fried potato > baTaaTa **mi2liyye,** min faDlak.
   1 grilled beef   2 ^raw meat^kibbe ...   3 baked chicken   4 boiled eggs^beeD   5 a lamb stew   6 fried eggplant^batinjeen

Expression^s 3ibaara^at	
cheers! (toast)	keesak^ik\kun
enjoy your meal (bon appétit)	Sa77teen

 13.6 What's the correct order in each column:

1	2	3	4
a la7m mishwe	a ba2leewa w 2ahwe	a jibilna yakhne	a keeskun
b kibbe nayye w 3ara2	b wajbe ra2isiyye	b liistit l2akl, 2iza bitriid	b nbiid 2abyaD, min faDlik
c lfetuura^bill	c mu2abbileet	c tfaDDalo, Sa77teen	c Taawle^table la kam shakhS^person?
d 2ahwe	d khallilak lbee2e	d ya m3allim	d liistit lmashruub

 13.7 Ask & answer: eg 2inta | hummus > shu bteekh**ud**? Sa7n **7ummuS,** |law sama7t^e\o|please
   1 2inte | fried eggplant   3 hiyye | chicken on rice   5 2inta | grilled lamb
   2 huwwe | baked fish   4 hinne | sweets and coffee   6 2into | glass of white wine

GRAMMAR

PRONOUNCING THE FEMININE a/e as it

RULE 13.8
The **e/a** feminine ending is pronounced as:
* **it** when in English **of** can be used eg siyyaara^car, but   siyyaarit lim3allim *the car of the teacher*^the teacher's car.
* **t** before a suffix   siyyaarto   *his car*.

 13.8 Say the following in Arabic, paying attention whether or not the end **it/t** should be pronounced:
   1 a bottle   2 a bottle of juice   3 my bottle   4 a cafe   5 her cafe   6 his sister's cafe.

13.9 Ask for: eg bottle of beer > **2anniinit biira,** 2iza bitriid.
   1 menu   4 chicken salad
   2 bottle of wine   5 fish soup *shoorba*
   3 flask *baT7a* 3ara2   6 piece *2iT3a* of baklava

UNIT 13

ee becomes ay

RULE 13.10 ee of a oneesyllable noun becomes **ay** when you add a suffix: eg b**ee**t, but b**ay**te

13.10 3abbo ljadwal*Fill in the table*:

	beet*house*	KheeT*string*	Zeet*oil*
eg my	bayte	kh...Te	z...te
our	...	...	...
your*m*	...	...	...
their	...	...	...

A DOUBLE CONSONANT IN THE MIDDLE OF A WORD

NOTE 13.11 Often, doubling the consonnant in the middle of a word means: **make** someone do something / something happen to someone/something

eg bfa**hh**mak means *I make you understand / I get you to understand / I explain to you.*

 13.11 What do the the following verbs mean?

1 lim3a**ll**im bi3a**ll**im ttlemiiz*students*. 3 lmijrim*criminal* kha**ww**af (fear) nnees*people*. 5 2ana bsa**mm**i3kun 3a ttisjiil*recording*.
2 samiir sha**rr**ab layla 3ara2. 4 samiir la**mm**a3 SibbaaTo lamma zaar layla. 6 lfarD bisha**ghgh**ilkun bi lbeet.

VERBS OF EXPRESSING

13.12 3abbo ljadwal*Fill in the table*:

	say	said	tell/speak	told/spoke
2ana	b2uul	2ilt	bi7ke	7kiit
ni7na	...	...	...	...
2inta	...	...	...	...
2inte	...	...	...	...
2into	...	...	...	...
huwwe	...	2aal	...	7ike
hiyye	...	...	...	7ikyit
hinne	...	...	...	7ikyo

 13.13 Ask: eg she | saying > shu 3am **bit2uul?**

1 he | said. 2 you*f* | saying. 3 she | said. 4 he | spoke Arabic. 5 they | are speaking Arabic. 6 you*m* | spoke Arabic.

UNIT 13

COMPREHEND & COMMUNICATE

13.14 tsamma3o w 7iTTo X bi l3amuud lmaZbuuT 3an samiir w layla:

	Sa7	ghalaT
a		
b		
c		
d		
e		
f		
g		
h		
i		
j		

13.15 ghayyro lkalimeet yalle bi khaTT ghaami2:

su2aal	jaweeb
shu **bjiblak**?	**Sa7n kibbe nayye** w kees **3ara2, min faDlak.**

13.16 You are the waiter/customer. Pretend that the vocabulary tables above are the menu. Interact with another person (real or imaginary) to order/serve.

13.17 7aDDro **sketsh,** fiya bideeye, mishikle w 7all.

13.18 t7addaso (tzakkaro l2as2ile w l2ajwibe):

1 greetings **2** feeling **3** nationality **4** address | phone no. **5** occupation **6** family **7** cafe **8** past activities **9** future activities **10** time | date | am doing **11** places | transport | directions **12** hotel **13 restaurant**

UNIT 14
How much are the shoes?

DIALOGUE

1 greetings | name **2** feeling **3** nationality **4** address | phone no. **5** occupation **6** family **7** cafe **8** past activities **9** future activities **10** time | date | activity now **11** places | transport | directions **12** hotel **13** restaurant **14** **shopping** **15** pastimes | taste **16** tourism | weather

1 S yoom ssabt bineesbik[suits you]?
2 L 2e ya 7abiibe[dear]. 2iza[if] min2uum[wake up] bakkiir[early] fiina na3mul kill shi 2abl lmasa w mnirja3[get back] mnirtee7[rest] mnii7.
3 S bije beekhdik ssee3a tmeene 2iza baddik.
4 L fikra[idea] mnii7a. heek[that way], minruu7 mnitrawwa2[have breakfast] mne2iish 2awwal[first] shi[thing].
5 S 2ahlik[parents] mle3iin ya layla. kint bfaDDil[prefer] 2inno ni7na nishitre[buy] lmashruub w hinne l2akl. byi7ikmo[dictate] shwayy.
6 L samiir, ma tballish[start] tinti2idun[criticise]. ba3d ma tjawwazna[get married] 7atta[even].
7 S Tayyib ma3leesh. bZammir[toot] w btinzale[come down], ma heek[not so]?
8 L 2e ma yhimmak[don't worry], Sirt 2inta mni l3ayle. rakhkhuule[loosen] l7abl[rope] shwayy.
9 S lakeen 2awwal shi ba3d ttirwii2a, minruu7 3a lmool[shopping centre], w minkhalliS[finish] bi ssuppermaarket.
10 L Sa7. 3milt liista la kill shi. ma ra7 nDayyi3[waste] wa2t 2abadan[at all]. 2awwal shi minruu7 3a ma7alleet[shops] lityeeb[clothes]. mnishitriilak l2amiiS[shirt] w lbanTaloon[trousers] w SSibbaaT yalle 2iltillak 7abbaytun. w ba3deen mnishitre lla7me w lkhiDra[vegetables] w lifweeke[fruit] w l7ilweyeet. w 2iza Saar[happens that] fi wa2t, minshuuf 2iza fi shi 3afsh[furniture] 7ilo. bas samiir ma 2iltille[tell], b2addeesh lkhaatim[ring] yalle shtaraytille yyee?
11 S 3ayb[shame] tis2aliine[ask] heek[such] su2aal. b2illik yimkin[maybe] ba3d kam[a few] sine[year] 7atta[so that] ma |yghiTT 3a 2albik|[faint] halla2. bas fiine[can] 2illik 2inno ma ra7 ni2dir[be able to] nishitre beet 2ariiban.
12 L ha...ha...! samiir, 2inta mabSuT[happy] 2adde[as much as me]?
13 S shu 2awlik?[What do you think]?

1 Does Saturday suit you?
2 Yes, darling. If we wake up early, we can do everything before the evening and get back and have a good rest.
3 I'll come and pick you up at eight if you like.
4 Good idea. That way, we'll go and have a herb-pizza breakfast before all else.
5 Your parents are crafty, Layla. I would've preferred us to buy the drinks and them the food. They do dictate a bit.
6 Samir, don't start criticising them. We haven't even got married yet.
7 OK. Never mind. I'll toot and you come down, yeh?
8 Don't worry, you're family now. They've loosened the rope around me a little.
9 So, first thing after breakfast, we'll go to the shopping centre, and we'll finish up at the supermarket.
10 Correct. I've made a list of everything. We're not going to waste any time. First, we'll go to the clothes shops. We'll buy you the shirt, pants and shoes that I told you I liked. Then, we'll buy the meat, vegetables, fruit and sweets. And if there's time, we'll see if there's any nice furniture. But, Samir, you haven't told me, how much was the ring you bought me?
11 Shame on you for asking me such a question. I may tell you in a few years, so that you don't faint now. But I can tell you that we're not going to be able to buy a house in the near future.
12 Ha ... ha ...! Samir, are you as happy as I am?
13 What do you think?

 14.1

1 2imtiin ra7 yitlee2o?
2 2ayya see3a byije byeekhida?
3 shu ra7 ya3imlo 2awwal shi?
4 la ween ra7 yruu7o ba3d ttirwii2a?
5 shu badda layla 2innun yishitro 2awwal shi?
6 lkhaatim ghaale 2aw rkhiiS?

UNIT 14

CULTURE

SPENDING

In Lebanon it is traditionally the male who pays for a woman when they go out. It also follows that a man's family pays for the engagement and wedding expenses.

Cost is closely associated with the display of happiness, public stature, and personal dignity. So, no expense is usually spared at a celebration. The lavish amount of sumptuous food and drink is usually a reflection of that. On those occasions, it can be difficult to tell whether or not the family is poor.

Likewise for physical appearance. As in many other Mediterranean cultures, much emphasis is placed on self-presentation in everyday life and especially at public occasions. It is not uncommon for women to go to the hairdresser's before attending church on a Sunday morning. And they do not need special events to wear the latest fashions. Let alone the attention given to beauty products and other forms of showy enhancements.

Men also feel pride in donning their best at public gatherings. Women may hint, or assist more assertively as to the man's choice of tie, colour and accessories.

VOCABULARY

SHOPPING ttasawwo2	
places	ma7alleet
shop//market/shopping centre/supermarket	dikkeen/ma7all//suu2/mool/suppermaarket

14.2 Ask: eg 2inta (shop) > la ween **raayi7**? (Choose: raayi7[m] / raay7a[f] / ray7iin[p])
   1 huwwe (shopping centre) 2 hinne (market) 3 2inte (supermarket) 4 2into (shop)

14.3 What are the answers to the exercise above? eg 2inta (shop) > **raayi7 3a ddikkeen.**

Supermarket suppermaarket	
soap/toothbrush/toothpaste	Sabuun/firsheeyit sneen/ma3juun sneen
butter/jam/bread	zibde/mrabba/khibz
apple/pear/orange/banana	tiffee7a/njaaSa/bird2aane/mawze sg tiffee7/njaaS/bird2aan/mooz pl
meat/veggies/fruit/cheese/sweets	la7m/khiDra/fweeke/jibne/7ilweyeet
rice/sugar/flour/canned foods	rizz/sikkar/T7iin/m3allabeet

 14.4 Ask: eg 2inta > **shu baddak tishitre?**
   1 hiyye 2 hinne 3 2inte 4 2into 5 2ana 6 ni7na

 14.5 Answer: eg badde 2ishitre (kilo of apples) > badde 2ishitre **kiilo tiffee7**.
   (Choose from: sha2fe[piece] loo7[bar] bakeet[packet] kiis[bag]
1 baddna nishitre (packet of butter)   3 baddak tishitre (kilo baklava)   5 baddik tishitre (toothpaste)
2 baddun yishitro (bar of soap)   4 badde 2ishitre (bag of rice)   6 baddkun tishitro (a piece of cheese)

UNIT 14

Clothes tyeeb/maleebis

shirt/dress/jumper/jacket	2amiiS/fisTaan/kanze/jakeet	sg
	2imSaan/fsaTiin/kanzeet/jaketteet	pl
pants/shorts/socks/shoes	banTaloon^eet/shoort^eet/kalseet/SibbaT^SbabiiT	

14.6 Answer: eg shu ra7 tjarrib^try on? (black shirt) > ra7 jarrib **l2amiiS l2aswad**.

(Choose the **colour**: 2aswad^sawda\suud *black* 2abyaD^bayDa\biiD *white* 2akhDar^khaDra\khiDr *green* 2azra2^zar2a\zir2 *blue*
2aSfar^Safra\Sifr *yellow* binne^iyye\iyye *brown* rmeede^iyye\iyye *grey* 2a7mar^7amra\7umr *red*)

1 shu ra7 yjarrib? (green jumper)   3 shu ra7 tjarrbe? (brown pants)   5 shu ra7 jarrib? (black shoes)
2 shu ra7 yjarrbo? (white socks)   4 shu ra7 tjarrbo? (blue dress)   6 shu ra7 njarrib? (yellow shorts)

Electrical appliances 2ajhize kahrabaa2iyye

| fridge/microwave/washing machine/dryer | birraad/maaycroweyv/ghisseele/nishsheefe |

14.7 Answer: eg shu naa2Sak^still in need of? (fridge) > naa2iSne **birraad**.
1 shu naa2So? (dryer)   2 shu naa2iSkun? (washing machine)   3 shu naa2iSun? (fridge)   4 shu naa2Sik? (microwave)

Electronics 2elektroniyyeet

| mobile phone/TV/ CD/DVD player | mobaayl/talfizyoon/ mshaghghil CD/DVD |

Furniture farsh

| bed/sofa/chair/cupboard/mirror | takht/kanabeeye/kirse/khzeene/mreeye | sg |
| | tkhuute/kanabeyeet/karaase/khazeeyin/mreyeet | pl |

14.8 Anwer: eg shu badd**ak** tjiib^get (mirror) > badd**e** jiib **mreeye**.
1 shu baddo yjiib? (chairs)   3 shu baddna njiib? (mobile phone) 5 shu baddak tjiib? (TV)
2 shu baddkun tjiibo? (beds)   4 shu baddik tjiibe? (sofas)

Verb\s fi3l \ 2af3aal

| buy/pay/cost | bishitre/bidfa3/bikallif^costs | present |
| | shtarayt/dafa3t/kallaf^cost | past |

14.9 Ask and answer: eg shu (you bought)? birraad. > shu shtarayt? shtarayt birraad.
1 shu (he bought)? kirse.   3 shu (you^m bought)? mreyeet.   5 2addeesh (you^m paid) 3a lkirse? khamsiin dolar.
2 shu (you^p bought)? takht. 4 shu (they bought)? kiilo tiffee7. 6 2addeesh (you^f paid) 3a ttakht? miit dolar.

14.10 Ask and answer: eg shtarayt ghisseele | tleet miit dolar > 2addeesh kalla**fitak**^cost you? kalla**fitne** tleet miit dolar.
1 shtara kirse | tisa3 dolaraat.   3 shtarayt khzeene | tleetaw sab3iin dolar.   5 shtarayna mreyeet | 3ishriin dolar.
2 shtarit kiilo tiffee7 | dolareen. 4 shtarit kanabeeye | tleetaw 2arb3iin dolar. 6 shtaro 2imSaan | tis3iin dolar.

Expression 3ibaara / 3ibaaraat

| I'm going shopping | raayi7 2ishitre kam gharaD |

14.11 Circle the word that does not fit in:
1 rizz zibde 7ilweyeet 2amiiS   2 tiffee7a njaaSa khzeene mawze   3 birraad talfizyoon SibbaaT mreeye
4 bishitre bi2ra bidfa3 bikallif 5 la7me khiDra fweeke mishwe   6 kalseet fisTaan mobaayl banTaloon

GRAMMAR

TO/FOR: 'l' before the verb's personal suffix.

14.12 See how the rule, note and reminder below apply to this table:

	PRESENT + l + personal suffix eg someone opens something **for** someone				PAST + l + personal suffix eg someone opened something **for** someone		
		for me/us	for you mfp	for him/her/them		for me/us	for you mfp	for him/her/them
2ana	bifta7	le|ilna	lak|lik|ilkun	lo|la|lun	fata7t	ille|illna	illak|illik|illkun	illo|illa|illun
ni7na	mnifta7	le|ilna	lak|lik|ilkun	lo|la|lun	fata7na	eele|eelna	eelak|eelik|eelkun	eelo|eela|eelun
2inta	btifta7	le|ilna	*lak	lo|la|lun	fata7t	ille|illna	*illak	illo|illa|illun
2inte	btifta7e	iile|iilna	*iilik	iilo|iila|iilun	fata7te	iile|iilna	*iilik	iilo|iila|iilun
2into	btifta7o	uule|uulna	*uulkun	uulo|uula|uulun	fata7to	uule|uulna	*uulkun	uulo|uula|uulun
huwwe	byifta7	le|ilna	lak|lik|ilkun	lo|la|lun	fata7	le|ilna	lak|lik|ilkun	lo|la|lun
hiyye	btifta7	le|ilna	lak|lik|ilkun	lo|la|lun	fata7it	le|ilna	lak|lik|ilkun	lo|la|lun
hinne	byifta7o	uule|uulna	uulak|uulik|uulkun	uulo|uula|uulun	fata7o	uule|uulna	uulak|uulik|uulkun	uulo|uula|uulun

RULE 14.12 To express **to / for**, you insert **l** before the verb's personal suffix.
  eg *He opened a bank account for you.* fata7lak\lik\ilkun 7seeb bi lbank.
*NOTE 14.12 (a) The 2nd person can only be reflexive, something one does to/for oneself (see asterix in table.)
  (b) The **l** is doubled in the **past** for **2ana** and **2inta** eg *I opened the door for you.* fatatillak lbeeb.
REMINDER Apply rule[see 11.14] when the verb ends in a vowel eg fata7o > fata7**uu**lak[ik\kun]

14.13 Ask: eg 2ilt[told] la[to] layla lkhabar[news] > shu **2iltilla?**
  1 jeebit la lbint[girl] 2akl.
  2 bteekhde la liwleed[children] hdiyye[present].
  3 rakhkhaSna[reduce] la layla ssi3r[price].
  4 7kiit la samiir l2iSSa[story].
  5 bi2ra la l3imyeen[blind] raseeyilun[letters].
  6 sama7o[permit] la samiir bi ssafar[travel].

ORDINAL NUMBERS   l2a3deed ttirtiibiyye

RULE 14.14
3rd to 10th: To form ordinal numbers, drop the cardinal number's vowels and initial 2aleef (if there is one) and use
  .ee.i (**.aa.i**[if guttural]) as the sound pattern:
    eg   tleete   >   tlt   >   **tee**l**i**t[m]   **tee**lt**e**[f]
         3ashra   >   3shr   >   3**aa**sh**i**r[m]   3**aa**shr**a**[f]
Word order: An ordinal number can go either **before or after** the noun:
  number > noun   eg khaamis marra[time] (number > noun **no agreement**) OR
  noun > number, using **the**:   eg lmarra lkhaamse   (noun > number **agreement**)
11th and beyond: the cardinal number goes after the noun, unchanged: noun + number, using **the**:
  eg lmarra[time] lkhamsaw 3ishriin[25th], shsheeri3 li7da3sh[11th]

14.14 3abbo ljadwal tteele[Fill in the following table].

CARDINAL				ORDINAL				
1	waa7ad	1st	2awwal/2awwle	11th	li7da3sh			
2	tneen	2nd	teene/teenye	12th	ttna3sh	20th	l3ishriin	21st	lwa7daw 3ishriin
3	tleete	3rd	teelit/teelte	13th	...tleetta3sh	30th	...tleetiin	32nd	...tneenaw tletiin
4	2arb3a	4th	...	14th	...2arba3ta3sh	40th	...2arb3iin	43rd	...tleetaw 2arb3iin
5	khamse	5th	...	15th	...khamsta3sh	50th	...khamsiin	54th	...2arb3aw khamsiin
6	sitte	6th	seedis/seedse	16th	...sitta3sh	60th	...sittiin	65th	...khamsaw sittiin
7	sab3a	7th	...	17th	...saba3ta3sh	70th	...sab3iin	76th	...sittaw sab3iin
8	tmeene	8th	...	18th	...tmeenta3sh	80th	...tmeniin	87th	...sab3aw tmeniin
9	tis3a	9th	...	19th	...tisa3ta3sh	90th	...tis3iin	98th	...tmeenaw tis3iin
10	3ashra	10th	...					100th	...miyye

14.15 Answer: eg 55th > bi shu 3am yi7tiflo[What are they celebrating]? bi zzikra **lkhamsaw khamsiin** [55th anniversary].
        1 3rd   2 7th   3 12th   4 31st   5 150th

UNIT 14

COMPREHEND & COMMUNICATE

14.16 tsamma3o w 7iTTo X bi l3amuud lmaZbuuT 3an samiir w layla:

	Sa7	ghalaT
a		
b		
c		
d		
e		
f		
g		
h		
i		
j		

14.17 ghayyro lkalimeet yalle bi khaTT ghaami2 :

su2aal	jaweeb
b2addeesh **l2amiiS**?	bi khamsiin dolar w sab3iin sant.

14.18 tbeedalo with a couple of other (real or imaginary) individuals about something you/they are wearing/have/own:
   eg   min ween sht**arayt 2alam**ak?   shtarayto min **lmaktabe**
        2addeesh kallaf**ak**?   kallafne **tleet** dolaraat w **3ishriin** sant.

14.19 7aDDro **sketsh,** fiya bideeye, mishikle w 7all.

14.20 t7addaso (tzakkaro l2as2ile w l2ajwibe):
   1 greetings   **2** feeling   **3** nationality   **4** address ... phone no.   **5** occupation   **6** family   **7** cafe
   8 past activities   **9** future activities   **10** time ... date ... am doing   **11** places ... transport ... directions
                     12 hotel   **13** restaurant   **14 shopping**

UNIT 15
What do you like doing in your spare time?

DIALOGUE

1 greetings | name 2 feeling 3 nationality 4 address | phone no. 5 occupation 6 family 7 cafe 8 past activities 9 future activities 10 time | date | activity now 11 places | transport | directions 12 hotel 13 restaurant 14 shopping **15 pastimes | taste** 16 tourism | weather

 samiir w layla

1 S layla, 2iza ra7 n2aDDe 3omirna[lifetime] sawa[together], leezim na3rif[know] shu kill waa7ad minna bi7ibb w ma bi7ibb, ma heek?
2 L 2e, Tab3an, samiir. 2ana b7ibbak 2aktar shi lamma bitkuun romantiike ma3e. shu bit7ibb ta3rif?
3 S badde 2a3rif, 2awwal shi, shu bit7ibbe ta3imle bi |wa2t lfaraagh|[spare time].
4 L shukran samiir 3a ha l2ihtimeem[attention]. 2ana b7ibb 2aktar shi l2akl bi lmaTaa3im w 2inne 2ishtre 2ishya 7ilwe ka tyeeb w mujawharaat[jewellery]. w b7ibb kameen seefir[travel] w zuur[visit] lma7alleet tteriikhiyye[historical]. bas ma b7ibb lfaTbool 2abadan[at all].
5 S 2inte mseefra |shi marra|[ever] 3a lkheerij[abroad]? raay7a[you've been], masalan[for example], 3a 2orooppa?
6 L la2, bas mseefra ma3ak ba3idma nitjawwaz[get married], Tab3an. raay7a 3a 2orooppa w |weenma|[wherever] bteekhidne[take].
7 S mnii7 2inne sa2alt[asked]. halla2 Saar fiina nkhaTTit[plan].
8 L 2eekil walla[or] raay7iin 3a maT3am?
9 S 2e 2eekil w sheerib ktiir. 2imme Taabkha 2ishya[things] ktiir Tayybe[tasty] lyoom. bas 2uliile[tell me] shu bit7ibbe kameen ta3imle ka hiweeye[hobby]?
10 L ma b7ibb ktiir 2ib2a[stay] bi lbeet. b7ibb 2iDhar[go out] shuuf 2aSdiQaa2e[friends] w ruu7 3a ssinama w 2itmashsha bi ma7alleet 7ilwe.
11 S |shi 3ajiib|[amazing], layla! 2ana hiweeyte kameen 2inne shuuf 2afleem. w |ma 3ada|[except for] lfaTbool, biftikir 2inno tnayneetna[we both] min7ibb nafs[same] l2ishya.
12 L ya3ne ra7 n2aDDe[spend] 2aw2aat[times] ktiir 7ilwe sawa 2abilma |yijiina wleed|[have children] w yilhuuna[distract].
13 S |bi l3aks|[on the contrary], layla, mneekhidun ma3na |weenma keen|[everywhere]. w killna mnimbiSiT[have a good time] sawa. |shu ra2yik|[what do you think]?
14 L nshalla heek ySiir[happen]!

1 Layla, if we're going to spend our lifetime together, we need to know what each one of us likes and dislikes, don't you think?
2 Yes, of course, Samir. I like you most when you're romantic with me. What would you like to know?
3 I want to know, first of all, what you like doing in your spare time.
4 Thanks, Samir, for this attention. The thing that I like most is eating in restaurants and buying nice things like clothes and jewellery. I also like travelling and visiting historical places. But I don't like football at all.
5 Have you ever been overseas? Have you been, for instance, to Europe?
6 No, but I'm travelling with you after we get married, of course. I'm going to Europe and wherever you take me.
7 Lucky I asked. Now we['re in a position to] can plan.
8 Have you eaten or are we going to a restaurant?
9 Yes, I've eaten and drunk a lot. Mum has cooked very nice things today. But tell me, what else do you like doing as a hobby?
10 I don't much like staying at home. I like going out to see my friends, going to the cinema and going for walks in nice places.
11 Amazing, Layla! My hobby is also seeing films. And apart from football, I think that we both like the same things.
12 That means we're going to have very good times together before we have kids and get distracted.
13 On the contrary, Layla, we'll take them with us everywhere. We will all have a good time together. What do you think?
14 I hope that's what happens!

 15.1

1 2imtiin layla bit7ibb samiir 2aktar shi?
2 shu baddo ya3rif samiir 3an layla?
3 shu baddo ya3rif samiir 3an safar[travel] layla?
4 leesh samiir mish ju3aan[hungry]?
5 layla w samiir bi7ibbo nafs l2ishya?
6 miin ra7 yeekhdo ma3un weenma keen?

UNIT 15

CULTURE

HOBBIES

In Lebanon, hobbies can be a mesh of art, folklore and sporting activities:

Soccer is among the most popular sports in Lebanon, although basketball and volleyball are also much enjoyed. Weightlifting has been popular with many Lebanese athletes since the mid-20th century, and the country has traditionally sent weight lifters to international competitions.

The country is endowed with several well-equipped ski resorts, and downhill skiing is popular among the wealthy, while windsurfing and kayaking are favoured pastimes among the younger generation. The untamed peaks and breathtaking scenery of the Lebanese Mountains contribute to the popularity of hiking expeditions and mountain biking.

Those who prefer to enjoy themselves indoors, engage in national folk arts such as dabke (the national dance), and zajal (a sung folk-poetry challenge, over a meza and a glass of 2arak). These and traditional arts and crafts help while away the time of many.

VOCABULARY

HOBBIES/INTERESTS	hiweeyeet
Hobby	**hiweeye^{et}**
	b7ibb / ma b7ibb:
hunting	SSeed
fishing	Seed ssamak
going to the movies	ssinama
playing cards	li3b lwara2
sports/music	rryaaDa / lmusii2a
listening to music	^{vb}2itsamma3 3a lmusii2a
gardening	shshighil bi lijnayne
drawing/painting	rrasm
learning languages	^{vb}2it3allam lighghaat
travelling	ssafar

 15.2 Ask: eg 2inta| hunting and travelling > **shu hiweeytak**?

1 hinne| playing cards and gardening   3 hiyye| listening to music and travelling   5 2inte| gardening and painting
2 2into| learning Arabic and playing sports   4 huwwe| playing music and drawing   6 ni7na| fishing and going to the movies

 15.3 What are the answers to the above exercise? eg 2inta| hunting and travelling > **b7ibb SSeed** w ssafar

 15.4 Negate the second part of 1-6 in the above exercise: eg **b7ibb SSeed**, bas ma b7ibb ssafar

 15.5 Answer for yourself: shu hinne hiweyeet**ak**? w shu ma bit7ibb ta3mul?

UNIT 15

FILM GENRE   noo3 lfilm ^{2afleem}

romance	b7ibb l2afleem: rromansiyye^{adj}
detective	lbulisiyye^{adj}
documentary	lwasee2iQiyye^{adj}
comedy	yalle bitDa77ik^{vb}
tragedy	yalle bit7azzin^{vb}
horror	b7ibb 2afleem: rri3bⁿⁿ
thriller/suspense	ttishwii2ⁿⁿ
adventure	lmughaamaraⁿⁿ
drama	ddraamaⁿⁿ

15.6 Answer: eg shu noo3 l2afleem^{films} yalle bit7ibba? (Di7k^{laughter}) > b7ibb l2afleem **yalle bitDa77ik**

1 shu noo3 l2afleem yalle bi7ibba? (3an TTabii3a^{nature})   4 shu noo3 l2afleem yalle ^{hiyye}bit7ibba? (fiya ktiir 7izn^{sadness})
2 shu noo3 l2afleem yalle bi7ibbuwa?(fiya makhaaTir^{risks})   5 shu noo3 l2afleem yalle min7ibba? (fiya ktiir 2a7dees^{action})
3 shu noo3 l2afleem yalle bit7ibbiya (fiya khoof^{fear})   6 shu noo3 l2afleem yalle bit7ibbuwa? (fiya jaraayim^{crimes})

15.7 Give a personal response to the question in the example of the above exercise.

GRAMMAR

THE PARTICIPLE

Definition: The participle is the verb form used with the auxiliary be/have eg I **am** sitt**ing**. I **have** eat**en**.

Usage: It is used to express: **ing**, replacing *3am* with verbs: -containing **no action** eg I am sitting *2ee3id*
                                                                                              -of **motion/travel** eg I am leaving *teerik*
                                      have in spoken Arabic   eg I have paid *deefi3*
                                      had in spoken Arabic   eg I had paid *kint deefi3*

RULE 15.8 Formation   Strip the verb down to its threeeconsonant root ie no prefix/suffix/vowels
                eg bi23ud^{I sit} > 23d   bitruk^{I leave} > trk   bidfa3^{I pay} > df3
Voweling   Place **ee** in the 1st syllable and **i** after the 2nd consonant eg 2ee3id, teerik, deefi3
Gender   Participles behave like adjectives eg (**mish**) seekin^m\seekne^f\seekniin^p, 2ee3id^{e\iin}, deefi3^{a\iin}

ing = 3am Sound pattern: .ee.i.

NO ACTION =state/condition =verbal adjective		MOBILITY/TRAVELLING		HAVE DONE	
Verb	Participle	Verb	Participle	Verb	Participle
I do	I am doing	I do	I am doing	I am doing	I have done
biskun *live*	seekin *living*	bitruk *leave*	teerik *leaving*	3am beekul *eating*	2eekil *eaten*
bi23ud *sit*	2ee3id *sitting*	bruu7 *go*	*raayi7 *going*	3am bidfa3 *paying*	deefi3 *paid*
bneem *sleep*	*neeyim *asleep*	birja3 *return*	reeji3 *returning*	3am biTrush *painting*	Taarish *painted*
bkhaaf *fear*	*khaayif *afraid*	bseefir *travel*	mseefir *travelling*		
biskut *fall silent*	seekit *silent*	binzal *stay*	neezil *staying*		
Syllables with **.i..a.** become **.i..een**		If the **present ends in a vowel,** the participle ends in **e**			
bin3as *feel sleepy*	ni3seen *sleepy*	bimshe *walk*	meeshe *leaving*		
bindam *regret*	nidmeen *regretful*	bib2a *stay*	bee2e *staying*		

*NOTE 15.8 If the verb only has two consonants, insert **y** as a middle consonant to make up the third.
         eg bneem is stripped down to **n m**. Add **y** = nym > .ee.i. = neeyim

15.8 eg 2ana (living) bi bayruut > 2ana seekin bi bayruut.
1 2inte (living) bi london.   3 hiyye (sleepy) ktiir.   5 ni7na (staying) bi l2oteel la tleet 2asabii3^{weeks}.
2 halla2 hinne (sitting) bi SSaff.   4 2into (travelling) 3a lyabaan. 6 2inta (have heard) 2inno^{that} libraziil balad 7ilo?

UNIT 15

15.9 What are the questions for the exercise above:
  eg 2ana (living) in bayruut. > ween **seekin?**
  2ana (going) to school. > [la replaces 3a in a question] la ween **raayi7?**

15.10 Using the participle, say in Arabic what five things apply/don't apply to you now.
eg I live in Beirut. I am sitting in the classroom [bi SSaf]. I am not sleepy. I am leaving here in [ba3d] one hour and going back home.

15.11 Choose the appropriate tense from the column on the right to fill in the gaps:
  eg **asleep** > [present]halla2 2inta neeyim | [past]lamma zirtak kint neeyim | [future]lamma bzuurak bitkuun neeyim

1 living
a huwwe ... bi beriiz
b ssine lmaaDye ... bi london
c ssine ljeey...bi sidni
2 sitting
a halla2 2ana ... bi SSaff
b l2usbuu3 lmaaDe bi ha lwa2t[time] ... bi SSaff
c l2usbuu3 ljeey bi ha lwa2t ... bi SSaff
3 sleepy
a ni7na halla2 mish ktiir ...
b mbeeri7 ssee3a 7da3sh bi lleel ...
c bukra ba3d ssee3a 7da3sh bi lleel ...
4 paid
a ma yhimmik[don't worry], 2ana ... lfetuura.
b ... lfetuura lamma 2ijit[came] layla ta tidfa3a
c bukra 2abil ma shuufa, ... lfetuura

2ee3id	
deefi3	
seekin	present
ni3seniin	
keen seekin	
kinna ktiir ni3seniin	
kint 2ee3id	past
kint deefi3	
ra7 ykuun seekin	
bkuun 2ee3id	
bkuun deefi3	future
minkuun ktiir	
ni3seniin	

THE PASSIVE

Definition: The subject is impacted by someone else's action / the situation:

Active verb	Passive	
	Verb	**Adjectival verb/Participle**
I do something to someone eg I injure someone bi**jra7**[root: jr7]	Someone does something to me eg I get injured bi**njiri7**	The state I'm in as a result eg I am injured ma**jruu7**

RULE 15.12
Alternatives: You can either use the **verb** or **adjectival verb/participle** to convey the passive.
Formation: Remove the vowels of the active verb and insert the following general sound pattern of the:
passive **verb**: present: Place **n** before the root **jr7**, the vowel **i** after the 1st consonant and **i** after the 2nd eg bi**njiri7**
         past: Place **n** before the root **jr7**, the vowel **a** after the 1st consonant and **a** after the 2nd eg **njara7t**
passive **adjective**: Place **ma** before the root **jr7**, and **uu** after the 2nd consonant eg **majruu7**

15.12 3abbo ljadwal. tba3o lnumuuzaj[Fill in the table. Follow the model].

		PRESENT			PAST	
	Active	Passive		Active	Passive	
		verb	adjective		verb	adjective
	I injure	I get injured	I am injured	I injured	I got injured	I was injured
		..n.i.i.	ma..uu.		n.a.a.	kint ma..uu.
2ana	bijra7	binjiri7	majruu7 majruu7a majru7iin	jara7t	njara7t	kint majruu7 majruu7a majru7iin
ni7na	mnijra7	...		...	...	kinna
2inta	btijra7	...		...	...	...
2inte	btijra7e	...		...	...	...
2into	btijra7o	...		...	...	...
huwwe	byijra7	...		...	...	...
hiyye	btijra7	...		...	...	...
hinne	byijra7o	...		...	...	...

UNIT 15

 15.13 tba3o lmasal^{Follow the example}.

	Present:			Past:		
eg 2ana	bisma3^{I hear}	binsimi3^{I get heard}	ma**s**muu3^{I am heard}	smi3t^{I heard}	**n**sama3t^{I got heard}	kint ma**s**muu3^{I was heard}
1 2ana	bisru2^{I rob/steal}	...	...	sara2t	...	...
2 hiyye	btiksur^{it breaks}	...	...	kasarit	...	...
3 2ana^f	^fbib3at^{I send}	...	...	ba3att	...	...
4 huwwe	byil3ab^{it plays}	...	...	li3ib	...	...
5 ni7na	mnib3at^{we send}	...	...	ba3atna	...	...
6 hinne	byishrabo^{they drink}	...	...	shirbo	...	...

ADVERB + ma > VERB

RULE 15.14 When an adverb of time is followed by a verb, they are separated with **ma**:
    lam**ma**^{when} | kill**ma**^{whenever/every time} | ween**ma**^{wherever} || Drop *b/m* of the present after: 2abil**ma**^{before} | ba3id**ma**^{after}

 15.14 Answer: eg 2imtiin beekul? (before going) > beekul **2abilma** ruu7.
1 2imtiin ma bishrab 2ahwe? (before I sleep^{bneem}).
2 2imtiin byeekul? (after returning) 3a lbeet.
3 shu biSiir^{happens} (every time she travels)? btinsiri2.
4 la ween mneekhud kalibna ma3na? (wherever we go).
5 2imtiin birtee7^{relax}? (when I'm) ti3been.
6 2imtiin bitneeme? (every time I'm tired) ni3seene.

COMPREHEND & COMMUNICATE

🔊 15.15 tsamma3o w 7iTTo X bi l3amuud lmaZbuuT 3an samiir w layla:

	a	b	c	d	e	f	g	h	i	j
Sa7										
ghalaT										

 15.16 ghayyro lkalimeet yalle bi khaTT ghaami2:

shu bit7ibb ta3mul bi wa2t lfaraagh?	b7ibb **li3b lwar2**
shu hiweeytak^{hiweyeetak}?	**2it3allam lighghaat**
shu noo3 l2afleem yalle bit7ibba?	b7ibb l2afleem **yalle bitDa77ik**

15.17 tbeedalo with a couple of other (real or imaginary) individuals information about three things you/they like doing in your/their spare time.

15.18 7aDDro **sketsh** fiya bideeye, mishikle w 7all.

15.19 t7addaso (tzakkaro l2as2ile w l2ajwibe)
1 greetings   2 feeling   3 nationality   4 address | phone no.   5 occupation   6 family   7 cafe   8 past activities   9 future activities   10 time | date | am doing   11 places | transport | directions   12 hotel   13 restaurant   14 shopping   15 pastimes | taste

UNIT 16
Where shall we go on our holidays?

DIALOGUE

1 greetings | name   2 feeling   3 nationality   4 address | phone no.   5 occupation   6 family   7 cafe   8 past activities   9 future activities   10 time | date | activity now   11 places | transport | directions   12 hotel   13 restaurant   14 shopping   15 pastimes | taste   16 tourism | weather

The alphabet was born in the Phoenician/Lebanese city of Byblos and was adopted and adapted by other cultures.

Phoenician -- c. 900 B.C.	⇐	⋖	⌐	△	ヨ	Y	I	⊞	⊕
Earliest Greek -- c. 750 B.C. (Western Variant) ⟵	A	B	⌐	△	E	⊣	Z	H	⊖
Etruscan -- c. 650 B.C. ⟵	A	⌠	⌐	⊲	⌐	⊣	I	⊟	⊗
Latin -- c. 500 B.C.	A	B	C	D	E	F	G	H	
C to G -- 3rd cent. B.C. Latin -- 1st cent. B.C.	A	B	C	D	E	F	G	H	
Latin -- Middle Ages	A	B	C	D	E	F	G	H	I
Some European Additions	À		Ç	Đ	É				Î

    samiir w layla

1 S layla, 2iza ra7 nSiir siwwee7^tourists bi lmista2bal^future leezim nitmarran^practise 2awwal shi bi baladna.
2 L shu ha lfikra^idea l3aZiime^great samiir! fiina nshuuf kill shi bi libneen 2abilma nseefir 3a lkheerij^abroad.
3 S Sa7. shu ra2yik^what do you think 2iza minballish bi bayruut w ba3deen minkammil^complete bee2e^rest libneen?
4 L fikra mnii7a, Tab3an. lakeen minballish bi l3aaSme^capital w ba3deen mna3mul lmudun^cities lbee2ye w DDiya3^villages.
5 S Tayyib, |heet ta|^let's nruu7 3a lmat7af^museum lwaTane^national ta neekhud fikra 3aamme^general 3an teriikh^history baladna. w ba3deen fiina nzuur lmawee2i3^sites tterikhiyye w lma3aalim^landmarks lbee2ye. shu ra2yik?
6 L yalla^let's go, lyoom TTa2s^weather ktiir 7ilo w mishmis^sunny. minruu7 3a waSat^centre limdiine ta nshuuf l2asaraat^ruins l2adiime yalle ktashafuwa^discover |min kam sine|^a few years ago.
7 S 2e, w 2aalo^said 2inno bukra TTa2s ra7 ykuun 3aaTil^bad. ra7 ykuun fi shite^rain w hawa^wind. 2afDal^better 2inno ma nkuun barra^outside. minruu7 3a lmat7af.
8 L 2e. w bi niheeyit l2usbuu3 fiina nzuur katidra2iyyit^cathedral mar^saint jiryus^George w ljeemi3^mosque likbiir yalle |7adda tameem|^right next to. hinne kameen bi waSat limdiine.
9 S layla, 2imtiin 2eekhir marra ri7te 3a ma3raD^gallery lfann^art? seemi3 2inno fi 3arD^exhibit la law7aat^paintings picaasso huniik. bit7ibbe heek shi?
10 L 2ana |bmuut bi heek shi|^I'd die for that sort of thing, samiir! Tab3an leezim nruu7.
11 S leezim ntalfin^phone w nis2al min 2ayya see3a la 2ayya see3a byifta7 lmat7af misheen^for bukra.
12 L samiir, sawa lyoom minshuuf libneen, w bukra l3aalam^world killo. 2afkaarak ktiir bti3jibne^like.
13 S layla, bas badde riDaake^satisfaction.
14 L ya 7abiibe, ya samiir!

1 Layla, if we're going to become tourists in the future, we should first get practice in our [own] country.
2 What a great idea, Samir! We can see everything in Lebanon before travelling abroad.
3 Correct. What would you say to starting in Beirut and then completing the rest of Lebanon?
4 A good idea, of course! So, we'll start with the capital and then do the other cities and the villages.
5 Ok. Let's go to the national museum to get a general idea about our country's history, and then we can visit historical sites and other landmarks. What do you think?
6 Let's go; today the weather is very nice and sunny. We'll go to the city centre to see the ancient ruins they discovered a few years ago.
7 Yes, and they said that tomorrow the weather was going to be bad. It's going to be rainy and windy. It would be better not to be outside. We'll go to the museum.
8 Yes. And on the weekend, we can visit Saint George Cathedral and the Grand Mosque which is right next to it. They're also at the centre of town.
9 Layla, when was the last time you went to the art gallery? I've heard that there is a Picasso exhibition there. Do you like that sort of thing?
10 I adore that sort of thing, Samir! Of course we should go.
11 We should call to find out the opening hours of the museum for tomorrow.
12 Samiir, together today we'll see Lebanon, tomorrow the whole world. I like your ideas very much.
13 Layla, all I want is for you to be happy.
14 I adore you, Samir!

 16.1

1 bi 2ayya balad ra7 yitmarrano^practise 3a lisyee7a^tourism?
2 2imtiin ra7 yzuuro DDiya3?
3 kiif TTa2s lyoom?
4 2imtiin ra7 yruu7o 3a lmat7af, w leesh?
5 shu fi 7add lkatidra2iyye tameem?
6 shu ra7 yshuufo ba3d libneen?

UNIT 16

CULTURE
TOURISM

The tourism industry in Lebanon has been historically important to the local economy, and remains to this day a major source of revenue for Lebanon. Before the Lebanese Civil War (1975-1990), Lebanon was widely regarded as "the Switzerland of the Middle East," and Beirut "the Paris of the Middle East," often cited as a financial and business hub where visitors could savor the Levantine Mediterranean culture and culinary delights. Since the end of the war, tourism has made a steady comeback.

Lebanon is considered to be a mosaic of cultural diversity, where the East and West meet in all their unique and historical richness. From Stone Age settlements to Phoenician city-states, from Roman temples to rock-cut hermitages, from Crusader Castles to Mamluk mosques and Ottoman hammams, the country's historical and archaeological sites are a true encyclopedia of ancient and modern world history.

VOCABULARY

TOURIST LOCATIONS   lmawee2i3 ssiyee7iyye

Landmark^s	ma3lam^{ma3aalim}
church	kniise^{kaneeyis}
mosque	jeemi3^{jaweemi3}
museum	mat7af ^{matee7if}
art gallery	mat7af fanne^{art}
exhibition	ma3raD^{ma3aariD}
statue	timseel^{tamesiil}
heritage building	mabna^{mabeene} turaase^{iyye}
historical site	maw2i3^{mawee2i3} teriikhe^{iyye}
ancient ruins	2asaraat 2adiime

 16.2 Ask and answer: eg tamesiil > badde shuuf **tamesiil,** la ween bruu7**?** ruu7 3a **lmat7af.**

1 2ahamm$^{most\ important}$ lmawee2i3.
2 lma7alleet ddiiniyye^{religious}.
3 hayeekil^{temples} rumeeniyye.
4 |lfann lmi3maare|^{architecture}.
5 |law7aat fanniyye|^{paintings}.
6 2ishya ma3ruuDa.

THE WEATHER TTa2s

It's good weather	TTa2s 7ilo
cloudy	mghayyim
sunny	mishmis
cold	fi$^{there\ is}$ bard
hot	shoob
windy	hawa
stormy	3aaSfe
raining	3am bitshatte
drizzling	3am bitshatte 3a lkhafiif
snowing	3am titluj

 16.3 Ask and answer: eg leebis^{wearing} shoort > kiif TTa2s lyoom? **fi shoob**

1 leezim 2ilbus kanze^{sweater}
2 fi shi 2abyaD^{white} 3am yinzal$^{come\ down}$
3 Taarit^{flew} birnayTte^{hat}
4 nballeet$^{I'm\ wet}$
5 3am bi3ra2^{sweating}
6 ra7 tshatte

UNIT 16

GRAMMAR
ROOT DERIVATIONS

NOTE 16.4 The consonantal root of a word gives its basic meaning. The vowels give the grammar and derivations. From the mostly threeeletter root, you can derive the noun, verb, person, place etc....

RULE 16.4 To strip a word down to its mostly threeeconsonant root remove all vowels, suffixes, prefixes, and one of the doubles if there is one, eg m3allim[teacher] becomes ~~m3allim~~ ie 3lm, which is to do with knowledge.

16.4   3abbo nnaa2iS [Fill in what's missing]:

consonantal root	noun	verb	person	place	passive
to do with			sound pattern (dot = consonant)		
			.ee.i.	ma..a.	ma..uu.
ktb	kiteebe	biktub	keetib	maktab	maktuub[letter]
writing		*I write*	*writer*	*office*	*written*
l3b	li3b	bil3ab	lee3ib	mal3ab	...
playing		*I play*	*player*	*playground*	*played*
3ml	3amal	ba3mul	3aamil	ma3mal	...
doing/working/making	*work*	*I work*	*worker*	*factory*	*done/made*
			.i..aa.		
...	Tabkh	biTbukh	Tibbaakh	maTbakh	maTbuukh
cooking		*I cook*	*cook*	*kitchen*	*cooked*
...	khabz	bikhbuz	khibbeez	furn/makhbaz	...
baking		*I bake*	*baker*	*baker's*	*baked*
...	Sarf	biSruf	Sirraaf	maSraf	...
spending		*I spend*	*teller*	*bank*	*spent*
			m.a..i.		
....	3ilm	bit3allam	m3allim		...
knowledge		*I learn*	*teacher*		*known*
....	maraD	bimraD	mmarriD		...
illness		*I get sick*	*nurse*		*diseased*
...	tiSwiir	bSawwir	mSawwir		
photographing		*I take a photo*	*photographer*		

16.5 Work out (a) the root and (b) the meaning of the words stemming from the same root:
1 sseekin byiskun bi maskan.
2 TTiyyarje biTayyir TTiyyaara min lmaTaar.
3 lfinneen bi7ibb lfann w bya3mul 2a3meel[works] fanniyye.
4 lamma 2raaybe[relative] shtara beet w 2arrab, Saar seekin ktiir 2ariib minne.
5 TTibbaakh bi7ibb TTabkh w byiTbukh ktiir bi lmaTbakh.
6 haydool ttameriin[exercises] bimarrnuukun la ti7ko 3arabe.

THE CONDITIONAL shsharT		
Tense	Situation	
Present	If we play tennis [may happen], I will win.	2iza mnil3ab[present] tenis, birba7[present]
Present	If we played tennis [is not happening], I would win.	law mnil3ab[present] tenis, kint birba7[present]
Past	If we had played tennis [didn't happen], I would have won.	law l3ibna[past] tenis, kint rbi7t[past]

16.6 rsimo diwwayra 7awla l3ibaara limneesbe been 2ooseen [Draw a circle around the appropriate phrase in brackets].
1 If you visited me, I would visit you.   (2iza bitzuurne, bzuurak || law bitzuurne, kint bzuurak || law ziritne, kint zirtak)
2 If you had visited me, I would have visited you.(2iza bitzuurne, bzuurak || law bitzuurne, kint bzuurak || law ziritne, kint zirtak)
3 If you visit me, I will visit you.   (2iza bitzuurne, bzuurak || law bitzuurne, kint bzuurak || law ziritne, kint zirtak)
4 If you drink, I will drink.   (2iza btishrab, bishrab || law btishrab, kint bishrab || law shribt, kint shribt)
5 If you had drunk, I would have drunk.   (2iza btishrab, bishrab || law btishrab, kint bishrab || law shribt, kint shribt)
6 If you drank, I would drink.   (2iza btishrab, bishrab || law btishrab, kint bishrab || law shribt, kint shribt)

UNIT 16

16.7 Say if it may happen/ is not happening/didn't happen:
eg law baddak tije, kint btije ma3e 3a l2ahwe. > You don't want to come = Is not happening
1. law bit7ibb lfann, kinna minruu7 sawa 3a lmat7af lfanne
2. lyoom fi shite w hawa; 2iza mniDhar[go out], minruu7 3a lmat7af, mish 3a l7adii2a[park].
3. 2iza bit7ibb l3ara2, minruu7 mnishrab kees.
4. law 2akalt kfeeye[enough], kint shbi3t[full].
5. 2iza btijo ma3e, minseefir bukra 3a shsheem[Damascus].
6. law shirbit, keenit ma 2idrit[able to] tsuu2[drive] ssiyyaara.

16.8 eg 2iza byis2al, (she|go) ma3o. > bitruu7
(Choose the verb to use: [get drunk]biskar [skirt]bshuuf [shift]bis2al [sa2alt]birja3 [rji3t]bit3allam [t3allamt][invite]bi3zum [3azamt]).
1. 2iza (she|invite|him), bi2uul '2e'.
2. law byishrabo, keeno (get drunk).
3. law (ask), keen 2ijeehun jaweeb.
4. law minseefir ma3o, kinna (come back) ti3beniin.
5. 2iza (you|learn) 3arabe, btit3allamiya bisir3a.
6. law (I|see) ha lfilm, kint 2iltillkun.

COMPREHEND & COMMUNICATE

16.9 tsamma3o w 7iTTo X bi l3amuud lmaZbuuT 3an samiir w layla:

	a	b	c	d	e	f	g	h	i	j
Sa7										
ghalaT										

16.10 ghayyro lkalimeet yalle bkhaTT ghaami2:

| la ween minruu7 **lyoom**? | |heet ta|[let's] nruu7 3a **lmat7af** |
| kiif TTa2s **lyoom**? | TTa2s 7ilo |

16.11 tbeedalo with a couple of other (real or imaginary) individuals the first three things you might do / places you might visit, if you go to Lebanon for the first time (see dialogue / table).

16.12 7aDDro **sketsh**, fiya bideeye, mishikle w 7all.

16.13 t7addaso (tzakkaro l2as2ile w l2ajwibe):
1 greetings   2 feeling   3 nationality   4 address | phone no.   5 occupation   6 family   7 cafe
8 past activities   9 future activities   10 time | date | am doing   11 places | transport | directions
12 hotel   13 restaurant   14 shopping   15 pastimes | taste   16 tourism | weather

ANSWERS & TRANSCRIPTS

1.1 1 2ismo samiir   2 2isma layla

1.2 1 Sabaa7 i lkheer / 2ahlan   2 2ahlan   3 masa lkheer / 2ahlan   4 ma3 i ssaleeme   5 ma3 i ssaleeme   6 ma3 i ssaleeme

1.3

			t	s	h	a	r	r	a	f	n	a
			m	a	s	a	l	k	h	ee	r	
			2	a	h	l	a	n				
			7	a	D	i	r	t	a	k		
S	a	b	aa	7	i	l	k	h	ee	r		

1.4 1 2isma   2 2isimkun   3 2ismun   4 2isimna   5 2ismik

1.5 1 2inta   2 ni7na   3 2inte   4 2ana   5 hinne   6 2into

1.6 1 shu 2isma?   2 shu 2ismun?   3 shu 2ismak?   4 shu 2isimkun?   5 shu 2ismo?   6 shu 2isme?

1.7 1 2isme layla   2 2isma 2elizabeet   3 2ismo 7abiib   4 2isimna tom w saam   5 2ismun 3ale w faaTme   6 2isme buTrus

1.8 1 w 2inte, shu 2ismik?   2 w 2into, shu 2isimkun?   3 w 2inta, shu 2ismak?
   4 w 7aDirtik, shu 2ismik?   5 w 7aDirtak, shu 2ismak?   6 w 2into, shu 2isimkun?

1.9 1 2ahlan   2 2ahlan/tsharrafna, (2ana) 2isme ...   3 2ahlan/tsharrafna, saam   4 ma3 i ssaleeme   5 ma3 i ssaleeme

1.10

		Sa7[true]	ghalaT[false]
a	hiyye 2isma faaTme		x
b	hiyye 2isma marii		x
c	hiyye 2isma layla	x	
d	huwwe 2ismo 7anna		x
e	huwwe 2ismo samiir	x	
f	hinne 2ismun 7abiib i w wafaa2		x
g	hinne 2ismun samiir i w layla	x	

2.1   1 mnii7a   2 mish ktiir mnii7. Saakhin shwayy.

2.2

How am I?		ne?
How are we?		na?
How are you? m		ak
How are you? f	kiif	ik
How are you? p		kun
How is he?		o
How is she?		a
How are they?		un

2.3   1 kiifkun?   2 kiifa?   3 kiifo?   4 kiifna?   5 kiifun?   6 kiifik?

2.4

FEELING	Adverb	Masculine	Feminine	Plural
well		mnii7	mnii7a	mnee7
very well	ktiir	mnii7	mnii7a	mnee7
not well	mish	mnii7	mnii7a	mnee7
a little tired	shwayy	ti3been	ti3beene	ti3ben**iin**
a little sick	shwayy	Saakhin	Saakhne	Sakhniin
so so	heek heek			

2.5   1 mish mnii7a   2 ktiir Saakhin   3 heek heek   4 ktiir mnee7   5 (ktiir) ti3beene

2.6

		Sa7	ghalaT
a	layla mish mnii7a		x
b	layla Saakhne shwayy		x
c	layla mnii7a lyoom	x	
d	samiir ktiir mnii7		x
e	samiir mish mnii7	x	
f	samiir ktiir Saakhin		x
g	samir shwayy Saakhin	x	

3.1   1 hinne libneniyye   2 huwwe 2ostraale / min 2ostraalya

3.2

balad[country]	mdiine[city] / 3aaSme[capital]	jinsiyye[nationality] / 2aSl[origins]		
		Masculine	Feminine	Plural
		Category 1		
2ostraalya	canbeera	2ostraale	2ostraliyye	
libneen	bayruut	libneene	libneniyye	
hollanda	2amsterdam	hollande	hollandiyye	
2irlanda	dablin	2irlande	2irlandiyye	
		Category 2		
2ameerka	washinton	2amerkeene	2amerkeniyye	2amerkeen
2almaanya	berliin	2almaane	2almaniyye	2almaan
lyabaan	tookyo	yabaane	yabaniyye	yabaan
SSiin	bejiin	Siine	Siniyye	Siin

ANSWERS & TRANSCRIPTS

3.3 1f 2a 3e 4c 5b 6d

3.4 1 braziile braziiliyye braziliyye   2 frinseewe frinsewiyye frinseewiyye   3 spanyoole spanyooliyye spanyool
4 ruuse rusiyye ruus   5 tilyeene tilyeniyye tilyeen   6 2ingliize 2ingliziyye 2ingliiz

3.5 1 hinne min ween? 2 2inte min ween? 3 huwwe min ween? 4 2inta min ween? 5 2into min ween? 6 ni7na min ween?

3.6 1 2ana yabaane.   2 ni7na 2almaan.   3 ni7na libneniyye.
4 huwwe 2irlande.   5 hinne 2ostraliyye.   6 2ana 2amerkeniyye.

3.7 1 2aSlun min ween?   2 2aSlik min ween?   3 2aSlo min ween?
4 2aSlak min ween?   5 2aSilkun min ween?   6 2aSilna min ween?

3.8 1 2aSle meksiike.   3 2aSilna 3ira2iyye   5 2aSlo frinseewe
2 2aSle nyuzilandiyye.   4 2aSla swisriyye   6 2aSlun yuneen

3.9 Feminine: hollanda siyyaara mdiine   Masculine: libneen 2ism balad

3.10

		Sa7	ghalaT
a	layla mnii7a	x	
b	samiir Saar 2a7san	x	
c	layla mish min hollanda	x	
d	layla min 2irlanda		x
e	layla 2ostraliyye bas 2aSla min libneen		x
f	tom min balad b3iid	x	
g	samiir w layla libneniyye		x

4.1 1 heek heek   2 ktiir mnii7   3 min sidni bi 2ostraalya
4 seekin bi raandwik, sheeri3 king, ra2im khamse   5 0415 736 298   6 3inweena w ra2m/numrit talifoona

4.2

٠	0	Sifir	١٠	10	3ashra				٢١	21	wa7daw 3ishriin
١	1	waa7ad	١١	11	7da3sh				٢٢	22	tneenaw 3ishriin
٢	2	tneen	١٢	12	tna3sh	٢٠	20	3ishriin	٣٣	33	tleetaw tletiin
٣	3	tleete	١٣	13	tleetta3sh	٣٠	30	tletiin	٤٤	44	2arb3aw 2arb3iin
٤	4	2arb3a	١٤	14	2arba3ta3sh	٤٠	40	2arb3iin	٥٥	55	khamsaw khamsiin
٥	5	khamse	١٥	15	khamista3sh	٥٠	50	khamsiin	٦٦	66	sittaw sittiin
٦	6	sitte	١٦	16	sitta3sh	٦٠	60	sittiin	٧٧	77	sab3aw sab3iin
٧	7	sab3a	١٧	17	saba3ta3sh	٧٠	70	sab3iin	٨٨	88	tmeenaw tmeniin
٨	8	tmeene	١٨	18	tmeenta3sh	٨٠	80	tmeniin	٩٩	99	tis3aw tis3iin
٩	9	tis3a	١٩	19	tisa3ta3sh	٩٠	90	tis3iin			

4.3 2addeesh: a sab3a naa2iS 2arb3a?   c tis3iin 3a tleete?   e tleetta3sh w tmeenaw 3ishriin?
b tmeene 3a tneen?   d khamse bi tmeene?   f tmeenaw sab3iin naa2iS tleetaw 2arb3iin?

4.4 1 ... bya3imlo 2arb3a   2 ... tleete   3 ... 3ishriin   4 ... sitte   5 ... khamsaw 3ishriin   6 ... khamsaw tletiin

4.5

١٠٠	100	miyye	٢٠٠	200	miteen	٣٠٠	300	tleet miyye
١٠١	101	miyye w waa7ad	٢٠٤	204	miteen w 2arb3a	٤٠٧	407	3arba3 miyye w sab3a
١٠٢	102	miyye w tneen	٢٠٥	205	miteen w khamse	٥٠٨	508	khams miyye w tmeene
١٠٣	103	miyye w tleete	٢٠٦	206	miteen w sitte	٦٠٩	609	sitt miyye w tis3a

4.6 a miyye w sab3a, miyye w tmeene, miyye w tis3a
b miteen w tleetaw tletiin, miteen w 2arb3aw tletiin, miteen w khamsaw tletiin
c tleet miyye w 3ashra, tleet miyye w 7da3sh, tleet miyye w tna3sh
d 2arba3 miyye w tis3a, 2arba3 miyye w 3ashra, 2arba3 miyye w 7da3sh
e khams miyye w tmeniin, khams miyye w wa7daw tmeniin, khams miyye w tneenaw tmeniin
f tisa3 miyye, tisa3 miyye w waa7ad, tisa3 miyye w tneen

4.7

١٠٠٠	1000	2alf	٢٠٠٠	2000	2alfeen	1m	malyoon	1b	milyaar
١٠٠١	1001	2alf w waa7ad	٢٠٠٣	2003	2alfeen w tleete	1m5	malyoon w khamse	1b7	milyaar w sab3a
١٠٠٢	1002	2alf w tneen	٢٠٠٤	2004	2alfeen w 2arb3a	1m6	malyoon w sitte	1b8	milyaar w tmeene
١٠٠٣	1003	2alf w tleete	٢٠٠٥	2005	2alfeen w khamse	1m7	malyoon w sab3a	1b9	milyaar w tis3a

4.8 1 ...? bi sint l2alfeen w tletta3sh.   4 ...? bi sint l2alf w tmen miyye w sab3aw 3ishriin.
2 ...? bi sint l2alf w tisa3 miyye w khamsaw 2arb3iin.   5 ...? bi sint ssitt miyye w tneenaw tletiin.
3 ...? bi sint l2alf w tisa3 miyye w tmeenaw 2arb3iin.   6 ...? bi sint l2alf w tmen miyye w wa7daw 3ishriin.

ANSWERS & TRANSCRIPTS

4.9

	Masculine				Feminine					
					siyyaara		shanta		dayne	
2ana		e	sheer3	e	siyyaart	e	shanitt	e	dayint	e
ni7na		na	sheeri3	na	siyyaarit	na	shantit	na	daynit	na
2inta		ak	sheer3	ak	siyyaart	ak	shanitt	ak	dayint	ak
2inte	3inween	ik	sheer3	ik	siyyaart	ik	shanitt	ik	dayint	ik
2into		kun	sheeri3	kun	siyyaarit	kun	shantit	kun	daynit	kun
huwwe		o	sheer3	o	siyyaart	o	shanitt	o	dayint	o
hiyye		a	sheeri3	a	siyyaarit	a	shantit	a	daynit	a
hinne		un	sheeri3	un	siyyaarit	un	shantit	un	daynit	un

4.10 1 hayda 2alamak 2 hayda kteebik 3 hayde shanitto 4 hayde siyyaarte 5 hayda kalibna 6 hayde zahritun

4.11 1 hayda kteeb miin? 2 hayde siyyaarit miin? 3 hayde zahrit miin? 4 hayda kalb miin? 5 hayda 2alam miin? 6 hayde shantit miin?

4.12 1 na3am, 2ana yabaniyye.   3 e, hiyye ti3beene.   5 na3am, 2ana 2ingliize.
2 la2, hayda mish kteebe.   4 la2, huwwe mish Saakhin.   6 la2, hayde mish shantitun.

4.13

		Sa7	ghalaT
a	layla ktiir mnii7a lyoom		x
b	tom heek heek lyoom		x
c	layla mish libneniyye		x
d	tom 2ingliize		x
e	samiir mish min melborn bi 2ostraalya	x	
f	tom seekin bi sheeri3 king ra2im sitte		x
g	layla ma^doesn't bta3Te samiir 3inweena	x	
h	samiir bya3Te ra2im talifoono		x

5.1 1 mnii7 2 (huwwe) m3allim 3 (byishtighil) bi madrase bi bayruut 4 (hiyye) Tibbaakha 5 (btishtighil) bi maTbakh 6 la2

5.2

Occupation	Masculine	Feminine	Plural
Teacher	m3allim	m3allme	m3allm**iin**
Artist	finneen	finneene	finneniin
Engineer	mhandis	mhandse	mhandsiin
Nurse	mmarriD	mmarrD**a**	mmarrD**iin**
Cook	Tibbaakh	Tibbaakha	Tibbakhiin
Hairdresser	7illaa2	7illaa2a	7illa2iin
Lawyer	mu7aame	mu7am**iyye**	mu7amiyye
Singer	mghanne	mghanniyye	mghanniyye

5.3 1 2ana mhandis. 2 2ana mmarDa. 3 ni7na mu7amiyye. 4 2ana finneen. 5 2ana mghanniyye. 6 ni7na 7illa2iin

5.4 m3allim finneen mmarriD Tibbaakh mu7aame

5.5

Person	Pronoun	Prefix	Stem	Suffix	Px	Stem	Sx	Px	Stem	Sx
			work			play			give	
1st	2ana	bi	shtighil		bi			b	a3Te	
	ni7na	mni	shtighil		mni			mn	a3Te	
2nd	2inta	bti	shtighil		bti			bt	a3Te	
	2inte	bti	shti**ghl**	e	bti	l3ab	e	bt	a3T	e
	2into	bti	shti**ghl**	o	bti		o	bt	a3T	o
3rd	huwwe	byi	shtighil		byi			by	a3Te	
	hiyye	bti	shtighil		bti			bt	a3Te	
	hinne	byi	shti**ghl**	o	byi		o	by	a3T	o

5.6 1 bishtighil ka Tibbaakha.   2 mnil3ab faTbool.   3 ma bta3Te ra2m talifoona.
4 bit3allam 3arabe.   5 byishtighlo ka mhandsiin.   6 byishtighil ka mu7aame.

5.7 1 shu byishtighlo? 2 shu btishtighil? 3 shu btishtighil? 4 shu mnishtighil? 5 shu btishtighlo? 6 shu btishtighle?

5.8 1 btishtighlo ka m3allmiin.   2 btishtighil ka finneene.   3 btishtighil ka mhandis.
4 mnishtighil ka mu7amiyye.   5 btishtighle ka mmarDa.   6 btishtighlo ka mghanniyye.

5.9

		Sa7	ghalaT
a	layla mnii7a	x	
b	samiir mish mnii7		x
c	samiir byishtighil ka Tibbaakh		x
d	layla btishtighil bi maTbakh	x	
e	layla bta3Te samiir 3inweena bas mish ra2m talifoona		x
f	layla ma bta3Te samiir 3inween bayta 2aw shighla bi hayde ssir3a	x	
g	barke lmarra ljeey		x

ANSWERS & TRANSCRIPTS

6.1 1 ktiir mnii7a   2 2e, hiyye min 3ayle kbiire   3 3inda tleet 2ikhwe w khams 2ikhweet
4 la2, huwwe min 3ayle zghiire   5 3indo bas khayy w 2ikhteen   6 seekniin bi zeet lbeet

6.2

Family member	Singular	Dual	Plural
Child	walad	waladeen	wleed
Brother	khayy / 2akh	khayyeen	2ikhwe
Sister	2ikht	2ikhteen	2ikhweet
Father	bayy / 2ab	bayyeen	2abaweet
Mother	2imm	2immeen	2immeet
Grandmother	sitt	sitteen	sitteet
Grandfather	jidd	jiddeen	jduud

6.3

					2	i	m	m
			k	h	a	y	y	
		2	i	k	h	t		

Adjective	Masculine	Feminine eg 3ayle	Plural eg 3iyal
Large	kbiir	kbiire	kbiire
Small	zghiir	zghiire	zghiire
Medium	mitwassiT	mitwassTa	mitwassTa
Only (child)	wa7iid	wa7iide	wa7idiin (people)

6.5
1 hinne ...? la2, hinne min 3ayle zghiire. 2 ni7na ...? la2, ni7na min 3ayle mitwassTa. 3 2into...? 2e, ni7na min 3ayle kbiire.
4 hiyye ...? la2, hiyye min 3ayle zghiire. 5 2inte ...? la2, 2ana min 3ayle zghiire. 6 huwwe ...? la2, huwwe min 3ayle zghiire

6.6 (a) **khayy**, khay**yeen**, tleet 2ikh**we**, 2arba3 2ikhwe, khams 2ikhwe, sitt 2ikhwe, saba3 2ikhwe, tmeen 2ikhwe, tisa3 2ikhwe, ...
2ikht, 2ikht**een**, tleet 2ikh**weet**, 2arba3 2ikhweet, khams 2ikhweet, sitt 2ikhweet, saba3 2ikhweet, tmeen 2ikhweet, ...
(b) 7da3sh**ar khayy/2ikht**, tna3shar khayy/2ikht, tletta3shar khayy/2ikht, 2arba3ta3sh**ar** khayy/2ikht, khamista3shar khayy/ ...
wa7daw 3ishriin khayy/2ikht, tneenaw 3ishriin khayy/2ikht, tleetaw 3ishriin khayy/2ikht, 2arb3aw 3ishriin khayy/2ikht, ...

6.7 1 ... 3ind**un**? 3indun **2ikht** wi7de.   4 ... 3ind**a**? 3inda **khayyeen**.
2 ... 3ind**na**? 3indna **tleet** 2ikhwe w sitt 2ikhweet.   5 ... 3ind**ik**? 2ana wa7iide.
3 ... 3ind**kun**? 3indkun **tleetta3shar** khayy.   6 ... 3ind**o**? 3indo khamsta3shar 2ikht.

6.8 1 l3inween 2 shsheeri3 3 rra2m 4 lim3allim 5 ssee3a^watch 6 shshighil^work

6.9		Sa7	ghalaT
a	layla mish ktiir mnii7a lyoom		x
b	layla min 3ayle ktiir zghiire		x
c	3inda tleet 2ikhwe w khams 2ikhweet	x	
d	samiir min 3ayle zghiire	x	
e	huwwe 3indo bas khayy w 2ikht		x
f	layla w 2ikhweeta killun seekniin bi zeet lbeet	x	
g	samir mish mal3un		x

7.1 1 meeshe l7aal   2 7ilwe   3 finjeen 2ahwe w saandwish faleefil
4 2iT3it ba2leewa w wi7de koola   5 byiTla3o bi 3ishriin dolar   6 la2, huwwe kariim

7.2 1 saandwish 2 shaay 3 7ilo 4 2akl

7.3 1 saandwish djeej, ...   2 tankit koola w 2iT3it ba2leewa, ...   3 finjeneen 2ahwe, ...
4 kibbeeyit 3aSiir ttiffee7, ...   5 tleet 2iTa3 7ilo, ...   6 2arba3 fnejiin shaay, ...

7.4	a	↓↓	beeb kbiir ^A big door	A fast car	siyyaara sarii3a
	the	↓↓	lbeeb likbiir ^The big door	The fast car	ssiyyaara ssarii3a
	is	↓↓	lbeeb kbiir ^The door is small	The car **is** fast	ssiyyaara sarii3a
	's/of	↓↑	beeb lghirfe ^The door of the room	The mother's car	siyyaar**it** l2imm
	our	↓↓	beeb ghirfitna ^The door of our room	Your mother's car	siyyaar**it** 2immak
	our	↓↓↓	beeb ghirfitna likbiir ^The big door of our room	Your mother's fast car	siyyaar**it** 2immak ssarii3a

7.5

A	B	A	B	A	B
a small family	3ayle zghiire	a great artist	finneen kbiir	a tired child	walad ti3been
the small family	l3ayle lizghiire	the great artist	lfinneen likbiir	the tired child	lwalad tti3been
the family is small	l3ayle zghiire	the studio is big	listuudyo kbiir	the child is tired	lwalad ti3been
the teacher's family	3aylit lim3allim	the artist's studio	stuudyo lfinneen	the child's toy	li3bit lwalad
your teacher's family	3aylit m3allmak	your artist's studio	stuudyo finneenak	your^m child's toy	li3bit waladak

ANSWERS & TRANSCRIPTS

7.6
1 fi shajra
2 hayde shajra kbiire
3 ween shshajra likbiire?
4 hayde shajrit 2immak
5 kiif shshajra? shshajra kbiire
6 fi shajrit 2immak likbiire

7.7

Pronoun	\multicolumn{12}{c}{b followed by vowel}	\multicolumn{9}{c}{b followed by consonant}
	P	Sm	Sx	P	Sm	Sx	P	Sm	Sx	P	Sm	Sx	P	Sm	Sx	P	Sm	Sx	P	Sm	Sx
	\multicolumn{3}{c}{drink}	\multicolumn{3}{c}{bill come to/go up}	\multicolumn{3}{c}{eat}	\multicolumn{3}{c}{take}	\multicolumn{6}{c}{would like}	\multicolumn{3}{c}{(will) be}
2ana	bi			bi			b	eekul		b	eekhud		b			b			b		
ni7na	mni			mni			mn	eekul		mn	eekhud		min			min			min		
2inta	bti			bti			bt	eekul		bt	eekhud		bit			bit			bit		
2inte	bti	shrab	e	bti	Tla3 bi	e	bt	eekul	e	bt	eekhd	e	bit	7ibb	e	bit	riid	e	bit	kuun	e
2into	bti		o	bti		o	bt	eekul	o	bt	eekhd	o	bit		o	bit		o	bit		o
huwwe	byi			byi			by	eekul		by	eekhud		bi			bi			bi		
hiyye	bti			bti			bt	eekul		bt	eekhud		bit			bit			bit		
hinne	byi		o	byi		o	by	eekul	o	by	eekhd	o	bi		o	bi		o	bi		o

7.8 2inte, 2into, hinne

7.9 a by b bi c by d by e bi

7.10 a bti b bit c bt d bt e bit

7.11 1 byishrab 2 byeeklo 3 bteekhdo 4 bteekhde 5 bikuun 6 byiTla3o bi

7.12 1 beekhud 2 mneekhud 3 beekhud 4 mneekhud 5 beekhud 6 beekhud

7.13
1 la2, ma beekul ...
2 la2, ma baddo ...
3 la2, ma byishtighlo ...
4 la2, ma bkuun ....
5 la2, ma beekhud ...
6 la2, ma bta3Te ....

7.14
1 la2, ma baddo ....
2 la2, hayde mish 2anniine, ...
3 la2, ma mnishrab ....
4 la2, hayde ssiyyaara mish 7ilwe, ...
5 la2, l7eeT mish 3ariiD, ...
6 la2, ma byiTlub biira, ...

7.15 1 fiik ti7ke 2 ra7 truu7 3 leezim yidfa3 4 bit7ibb teekul 5 bi7ibbo yeeklo ... 2abilma yneemo 6 ra7 na3Te

7.16

	PRESENT	\multicolumn{3}{c}{IMPERATIVE}
	You	MASCULINE	FEMININE	PLURAL
	bit7ibb like/love	bit7ibb	bit7ibbe	bit7ibbo
	bitruu7 go	ruu7	ruu7e	ruu7o
	bitfuut enter	fuut	fuute	fuuto
	bitjiib bring	jiib	jiibe	jiibo
	btitfaDDal here you are/invite sone to do sthg	tfaDDal	tfaDDale	tfaDDalo
	btitTalla3 look	tTalla3	tTalla3e	tTalla3o
mid a	btishrab drink	btishraab	btishrabe	btishrabo
	btiw2af stop/stand	w2aaf	w2afe	w2afo
mid u	bteekul eat	bteekool	kile	kilo
	bta3mul do	bta3mool	3mile	3milo
ending in a	bti2ra read	bti2raa	2ri	2ru
	btighfa fall asleep	ghfaa	ghfi	ghfu
ending in e	btishitre	btishtrii	shtri	shtru
	bta3Te	bta3Tii	3Ti	3Tu

7.17 1 7amme 2 2aTTi3 3 7iTT 4 di22e 5 7iTTe 6 ksire 7 khliTo 8 Diifo 9 kitto 10 2libo

7.18

	Adjective	Masculine	Feminine	Plural
Please	Present	2iza bitriid	2iza bitriide	2iza bitriido
	Possessive ending	min faDlak	min faDlik	min faDilkun
	Imperative	3mool ma3ruuf	3mile ma3ruuf	3milo ma3ruuf

7.19
1 ma ti23ud lakeen.
2 ma tisra3e lakeen.
3 ma tneemo lakeen.
4 ma tishrabo lakeen.
5 ma teekle lakeen.
6 ma tseefro lakeen.

7.20

		Sa7	ghalaT
a	layla bit7ibb l2ahwe	x	
b	layla badda 2anniinit koola		x
c	layla badda finjeen 2ahwe w saandwish faleefil	x	
d	samiir bi3ayyiT la rrijeel	x	
e	samiir baddo 2iT3it ba2leewa w tankit koola		x
f	l2akl w lmashruub byiTla3o bi 3ashr dolaraat		x

ANSWERS & TRANSCRIPTS

8.1 1 ktiir mabSuuT.   3 2aal 'trawwa2t mne2iish'.   5 seekne bisheeri3 lmistashfa.
2 niheeyit 2usbuu3o keenit ktiir 7ilwe.   4 2aalit 'ntabaht la 2imme'.   6 2aal 'b7ibb 2itmashsha…'.

8.3

	contacted	swam	helped	travelled	went for a walk	bought	did	drank	played	visited	went	saw	was	read
2ana	ttaSalt[hi]	saba7t	see3adt	seefart[3a]	tmashshayt	shtarayt	3milt	shribt	l3ibt	khift	ri7t[3a]	shift	kint	2riit
ni7na	ttaSalna	saba7na	see3adna	seefarna	tmashshayna	shtarayna	3milna	shribna	l3ibna	khifna	ri7na	shifna	kinna	2riina
2inta	ttaSalt	saba7t	see3adt	seefart	tmashshayt	shtarayt	3milt	shribt	l3ibt	khif	ri7t	shift	kint	2riit
2inte	ttaSalte	saba7te	see3adte	seefarte	tmashshayte	shtarayte	3milte	shribte	l3ibte	khifte	ri7te	shifte	kinte	2riite
2into	ttaSalto	saba7to	see3adto	seefarto	tmashshayto	shtarayto	3milto	shribto	l3ibto	khifto	ri7to	shifto	kinto	2riito
huwwe	ttaSal	saba7	see3ad	seefar	tmashsha	shtara	3imil	shirib	li3ib	khaaf	raa7	sheef	keen	2ire
hiyye	ttaSalit	saba7it	see3adit	seefarit	tmashshit	shtarit	3imlit	shirbit	li3bit	khaafit	raa7it	sheefit	keenit	2iryit
hinne	ttaSalo	saba7o	see3ado	seefaro	tmashsho	shtaro	3imlo	shirbo	li3bo	khaafo	raa7o	sheefo	keeno	2iryo

8.4 1 shu 3milte l2usbuu3 lmaaDe?   3 shu 3imil l2usbuu3 lmaaDe?   5 shu 3milto ssine lmaaDye?
2 shu 3imlit bi niheeyit l2usbuu3?   4 shu 3imlo bi niheeyit l2usbuu3?   6 shu 3imlit shshahr lmaaDe?

8.5
1 l2usbuu3 lmaaDe ma saba7t[f] ma3 2aSdiQaa2e.   3 ma sheef film 7ilo l2usbuu3 lmaaDe.   5 ma seefarna 3a libneen ssine[year] lmaaDye.
2 ma 2akalit ktiir bi niheeyit l2usbuu3.   4 ma see3ado 2immun bi niheeyit l2usbuu3.   6 ma 2iryit meeri kteeb 7ilo shshahr[month] lmaaDe.

8.6

		Sa7	ghalaT
a	samiir ma keen mabSuuT bi niheeyit l2usbuu3		x
b	samir trawwa2 saandwish faleefil		x
c	layla keenit ktiir mabSuuTa yoom ssabt		x
d	2imma la layla keenit mariiDa	x	
e	layla 2akhadit 2imma 3a lmistashfa	x	
f	samiir ma bi7ibb yitmashsha bisheeri3 lmistashfa		x

9.1 1 ktiir mabSuuT   2 samiir bizarrik la layla   3 2aal, 'ra7 ruu7 2isba7 ma3 Sadii2e kariim'
4 li2anno 2imma mariiDa/Saakhne   5 bitruu7 3a ljabal   6 ta tSi77 2imma

9.2

	Singular	Plural	
		Things fem. = plural	**People** masc. & fem.
Fast slow	sarii3 baTii2	sarii3**a** baTii2**a**	sari3**iin** baTi2**iin**
Beautiful ugly	7ilo bishi3	7ilw**e** bish3**a**	7ilw**iin** bish3**iin**
Interesting boring	7ilo mumill	7ilw**e** mumill**e**	7ilw**iin** mumill**iin**
Happy unhappy	mabSuuT ta3iis	mabSuuT**a** ta3iis**e**	mabSuT**iin** ta3is**iin**
			ee(**aa** if guttural/end in r)
A little a lot	2aliil ktiire	2aliil**e** ktiir**e**	2l**ee**l kt**aar**
Near far	2ariib b3iid	2ariib**e** b3iid**e**	2r**aa**b b3**aa**d
New old	jdiid 3atii2	jdiid**e** 3atii2**a**	jd**ee**d 3t**ee**2
Long/tall short	Tawiil 2aSiir	Tawiil**e** 2aSiir**e**	Tw**aa**l 2S**aa**r
Clean dirty	nDiif wisikh	nDiif**e** wiskh**a**	nD**aa**f wiskh**iin**
Nice nasty	laTiif la2iim	laTiif**e** la2iim**e**	.u.a.a luTafa lu2ama
Generous stingy	kariim bakhiil	kariim**e** bakhiil**e**	kurama bukhala
Rich poor	ghane fa2iir	ghan**iyye** fa2iir**a**	.a..i.a 2aghniya fu2ara
Intelligent stupid	zake mahbuul	zak**iyye** mahbuul**e**	2azkiya mhebiil

9.3 1 kiif keenit l2afleem?   3 kiif keeno lim3allmiin?   5 kiif keenit li2leem?
2 kiif keenit libyuut?   4 kiif keeno nnees?   6 kiif keeno l2aSdiQaa2?

9.4 1 mish jdiide   2 ktiir 3atii2a   3 mish ktiir mabSutiin   4 shwayy lu2ama   5 ktaar   6 2aliile

9.5

PRESENT	beekul	[go]bruu7[3a]	bsee3id	bittiSil[bi]	bisba7	bseefir[3a]	ba3mul	bishrab	bil3ab	bi2ra
	FUTURE: ra7 …									
2ana	2eekul	ruu7	see3id	2ittiSil	2isba7	seefir	2a3mul	2ishrab	2il3ab	2i2ra
ni7na	neekul	nruu7	nsee3id	nittiSil	nisba7	nseefir	na3mul	nishrab	nil3ab	ni2ra
2inta	teekul	truu7	tsee3id	tittiSil	tisba7	tseefir	ta3mul	tishrab	til3ab	ti2ra
2inte	teekle	truu7e	tsee3de	tittiSle	tisba7e	tseefre	ta3mle	tishrabe	til3abe	ti2re
2into	teeklo	truu7o	tsee3do	tittiSlo	tisba7o	tseefro	ta3mlo	tishrabo	til3abo	ti2ro
huwwe	yeekul	yruu7	ysee3id	yittiSil	yisba7	yseefir	ya3mul	yishrab	yil3ab	yi2ra
hiyye	teekul	truu7	tsee3id	tittiSil	tisba7	tseefir	ta3mul	tishrab	til3ab	ti2ra
hinne	yeeklo	yruu7o	ysee3do	yittiSlo	yisba7o	yseefro	ya3mlo	yishrabo	yil3abo	yi2ro

9.6 1 shu ra7 ya3mul l2usbuu3 ljeey?   3 shu ra7 ya3imlo bi niheeyit l2usbuu3 ljeey?   5 shu ra7 ta3imlo bi niheeyit l2usbuu3 ljeey?
2 shu ra7 na3mul l2usbuu3 ljeey?   4 shu ra7 ta3mul l2usbuu3 ljeey?   6 shu ra7 ta3imle bi niheeyit l2usbuu3 ljeey?

ANSWERS & TRANSCRIPTS

9.7 1 ra7 see3id jaare binna2l. 2 ra7 2ittiSil bi 2aSdiQaa2e. 3 ra7 na3mul fariDna.
4 ra7 yishrabo 2ahwe ma3 sittun. 5 ra7 2i2ra kteeb ktiir 7ilo. 6 ra7 seefir 3a maSr.

9.8

	present	past	future
2ana	ma beekul	ma 2akalt	ma/mish ra7 2eekul
ni7na	ma mneekul	ma 2akalna	ma/mish ra7 neekul
2inta	ma bteekul	ma 2akalt	ma/mish ra7 teekul
2inte	ma bteekle	ma 2akalte	ma/mish ra7 teekle
2into	ma bteeklo	ma 2akalto	ma/mish ra7 teeklo
huwwe	ma byeekul	ma 2akal	ma/mish ra7 yeekul
hiyye	ma bteekul	ma 2akalit	ma/mish ra7 teekul
hinne	ma byeeklo	ma 2akalo	ma/mish ra7 yeeklo

9.9 1 ma bitsee3id khayya bi shighlo. 3 ma 2akal kill ssaandwish. 5 ma fiine 2a3mul farDe.
2 ma ttaSalo bi 2immun. 4 ma/mish ra7 ni2dir nruu7 ma3kun. 6 ma/mish ra7 truu7 tisba7 ma3a.

9.10

		Sa7	ghalaT
a	samir mish mabSuuT lyoom		x
b	ra7 ya3mul 2ishya 7ilwe l2usbuu3 ljeey	x	
c	bas layla ra7 tinzirib bi lbeet	x	
d	samiir ra7 yirtee7 w yi7Dar lfaTbool nhaar ssabt		x
e	3aylit layla bitruu7 3aadatan 3a ljabal	x	
f	ra7 yruu7o 3a ljabal bi niheeyit l2usbuu3 ljeey		x
g	layla badda 2inno samiir yzuurun w yeekhud la 2imma zhuur		x

10.1 1 li2anno layla btikhlaS mit2akhkhra 4 keen bi sab3a shshahr
2 btikhlaS ssee3a sab3a lmasa 5 la2, baddo yitlee2a ma3a bukra
3 bi 3ashra shshahr 6 ssee3a sitte w rib3 lmasa

10.2 1 ssee3a 7da3sh w rib3 (SSib7) 4 ssee3a sab3a 2illa tilt (lmasa)
2 ssee3a tinteen w tilt (ba3d DDohr) 5 ssee3a tna3sh 2illa rib3 (bi lleel)
3 ssee3a tleete w niSS 2illa khamse (ba3d DDohr) 6 ssee3a sitte 2illa khamse (SSib7)

10.3 1 ljim3a 2 ttaneen 3 lkhamiis 4 ssabt 5 l2irb3a 6 ttaleeta

10.4 1 lyoom bi tis3a niseen, 2alfeen 4 lyoom bi tleetaw 3ishriin tishriin l2awwal, 2alfeen w khamse
2 lyoom bi waa7ad 2ayluul, 2alfeen w tna3sh 5 lyoom bi tletta3sh 2ayyaar, 2alf w tisa3 miyye w khamsta3sh
3 lyoom bi tletiin kenuun tteene, 2alfeen w 3ashra 6 lyoom bi khamsaw 3ishriin kenuun l2awwal, 2alfeen w tleetta3sh

10.6 1 7zayraan, tammuuz w 2aab 2 2adaar, niseen w 2ayyaar
3 kenuun l2awwal, kenuun tteene w shbaaT 4 2ayluul, tishriin l2awwal w tishriin tteene

10.7 1 bi (faSl) SSeef 2 bi (faSl) shshite 3 bi (faSl) rrabii3 4 bi (faSl) lkhariif 5 bi (faSl) rrabii3 6 bi (faSl) lkhariif

10.8 1 bi (faSl) shshite 2 bi (faSl) SSeef 3 bi (faSl) lkhariif 4 bi (faSl) rrabii3 5 bi (faSl) SSeef 6 bi (faSl) shshite

10.9 1 min tleet tiyyeem, nhaar ttaneen, bi tleete kenuun tteene, ssee3a khamse w khamse SSib7
2 ba3d bukra, nhaar l2a7ad, bi tletta3sh 2ayyaar, ssee3a 2arb3a 2illa tilt ba3d DDohr
3 mbeeri7, nhaar lkhamiis, bi wa7daw 3ishriin tishriin l2awwal, ssee3a sab3a w rib3 lmasa

10.10 1 b2addeesh shshahr lyom? 4 b2addeesh shshahr ra7 ykuun ba3d bukra?
2 b2addeesh shshahr ra7 ykuun bukra? 5 b2addeesh shshahr keen ttaneen lmaaDe?
3 b2addeesh shshahr keen 2awwilt mbeeri7? 6 b2addeesh shshahr ra7 ykuun l2a7ad ljeey?

10.12

S¹	S	ee	f²			s³		b⁴
			a			h		a
			S		t⁵		s		3
t⁶	t	a	l	ee	t	a	h		d
					a		i		b
			2⁷		n		t		u
			a		ee		e		k
b⁸			y		n				r
u			l						a
k⁹	e	n	uu	n	t	t	ee	n¹⁰	e
r			l¹¹	ee	l			h	
a								aa	
			2¹²	a	d	aa	r		

10.13 1 shu 3am ya3imlo? 3 shu 3am ta3imle? 5 shu 3am ta3mul?
2 shu 3am ta3mul? 4 shu 3am ya3mul? 6 shu 3am ta3imlo?

10.14 1 3am beekul saandwish 3 3am ni2ra kteeb 5 3am ya3mul farDo
2 3am bishrab 3aSiir 4 3am nit3allam 3arabe 6 3am tiktub 3arabe

10.15 1 ma/mish 3am beekul saandwish jibne. 3 ma/mish 3am bishrab biira. 5 ma/mish 3am bitfarraj 3a ttalfizyoon.
2 3am bitnaffas^breathing hawa^air. 4 3am bit3allam 3arabe. 6 3am bi7ke w biktub bi l3arabe.

ANSWERS & TRANSCRIPTS

10.16

		Sa7	ghalaT
a	layla mashghuule ktiir bi ha l2iyyeem	x	
b	layla 3am tishtighil shwayy		x
c	2imm layla ba3da mariiDa	x	
d	layla ra7 tikhlaS mit2akhkhra bukra		x
e	ra7 yitlee2o ba3d bukra		x
f	lyoom bi sab3a shshahr		x

11.1 **1** yoom ssabt ljeey sse3a tleete w niSS. **2** byeekhud lbooSTa. **3** 2abl lmadrase bi shwayy
4 ra7 yit3arraf 3a kill 3aylit layla: 2imma w bayya w 2ikhiwta. **5** 2e. **6** li2anno naZar 2imma ktiir 2awe.

11.2 **1** la ween biruu7 ta yit3allam 3arabe? **3** 2immun mariiDa, la ween biruu7o? **5** la ween bitruu7 ta tseefir bi ttreen?
2 la ween biruu7o ta yishitro kteeb? **4** nsara2na, la ween minruu7? **6** la ween bitruu7 ta teekhud TTiyyaara?

11.3 **1** ruu7 3a lmadrase/ljeem3a. **3** ruu7o 3a lmistashfa. **5** ruu7 3a m7aTTit ttreen.
2 ruu7o 3a lmaktabe. **4** ruu7o 3a makhfar shshirTa. **6** ruu7e 3a lmaTaar.

11.4 **1** kiif bitruu7 3a lmadrase? **3** kiif bitruu7o 3a ljeem3a? **5** kiif minruu7 3a libraziil?
2 kiif biruu7o 3a lmistashfa? **4** kiif biruu7 3a lmaTaar? **6** kiif bitruu7e 3a ssuu2?

11.5 **1** ruu7e mashe. **2** ruu7o bi ttaksi. **3** ruu7o bi lbaaS. **4** ruu7 bi lmarkab. **5** ruu7o bi TTiyyaara. **6** ruu7e 3a lbisikleet.

11.6 **1** ruu7 mashe. **3** ruu7o/liffo 3a lyasaar/lishmeel. **5** khido lbaaS w nzalo 3ind lmaktabe.
2 khide taksi. **4** ruu7/liff 3a lyamiin. **6** 2Ta3e TTarii2.

11.7 **1** 2iddeem **2** wara **3** 2abl **4** 7add **5** ba3d **6** 2iddeem

11.8 liffe 3a lyasaar/lishmeel. khide lbaaS ra2im 3ashra. nzale 3ind lmadrase. ruu7e bi ttaksi la ljeem3a. mshi jeelis 7atta tuuSale 3a lmistashfa.

11.9 **1** kiif byijo? **2** kiif btijo? **3** kiif btije? **4** kiif mnije? **5** kiif btije? **6** kiif byije?

11.10 **1** ta3o bi ttaksi. **2** ta3o bi TTiyyaara. **3** ta3e mashe. **4** ta3o 3a lmotorsiikl. **5** ta3e bi lbaaS. **6** ta3a bi ttreen.

11.11

	Present continuous (**am doing**)	Past continuous (**was doing**)	Future continuous (**am going to\will be doing**)	
2ana	*I am eating* **3am** beekul	*I was eating* **kint 3am** beekul	*I am going to be* **ra7 kuun 3am** beekul	*I will be eating* **bkuun 3am** beekul
ni7na	3am neekul	kinna 3am neekul	ra7 nkuun 3am neekul	minkuun 3am neekul
2inta	3am teekul	kint 3am teekul	ra7 tkuun 3am teekul	bitkuun 3am teekul
2inte	3am teekle	kinte 3am teekle	ra7 tkuune 3am teekle	bitkuune 3am teekle
2into	3am teeklo	kinto 3am teeklo	ra7 tkuuno 3am teeklo	bitkuuno 3am teeklo
huwwe	3am yeekul	keen 3am yeekul	ra7 ykuun 3am yeekul	bikuun 3am yeekul
hiyye	3am teekul	keenit 3am teekul	ra7 tkuun 3am teekul	bitkuun 3am teekul
hinne	3am yeeklo	keeno 3am yeeklo	ra7 ykuuno 3am yeeklo	bikuuno 3am yeeklo

11.12 **1** shu keenit 3am ta3mul sse3a tleete? **4** shu keen 3am ya3mul sse3a sitte?
2 shu minkuun 3am na3mul sse3a tis3a? **5** shu kinto 3am ta3imlo sse3a tna3sh?
3 shu ra7 tkuun 3am ta3mul sse3a sab3a? **6** shu ra7 ykuuno 3am ya3imlo sse3a tinteen?

11.13 **1** keenit 3am ta3mul farDa. **3** ra7 kuun 3am beekul. **5** kinna 3am nil3am tenis.
2 minkuun 3am nishrab. **4** keen 3am yisba7. **6** ra7 ykuuno 3am yishtighlo.

11.14

		verbs ending in a:					
	consonant	vowel					
		a		**o**		**e**	
		lee2**a**	khahb**ba**	7abb**o**	sa2al**o**	bta3T**e**	bitna22**e**
jeeb	ne	ne	khabbeene	7abbuune	sa2aluune	bta3Tiine	bitna22iine
	na	na	khabbeena	7abbuuna	sa2aluuna	bta3Tiina	bitna22iina
	ak	k	khabbeek	7abbuuk	sa2aluuk	bta3Tiik	bitna22iik
	ik	ke	khabbeeke	7abbuuke	sa2aluuke	bta3Tiike	bitna22iike
	kun	kun	khabbeekun	7abbuukun	sa2aluukun	bta3Tiikun	bitna22iikun
	o		khabbee	7abbuu	sa2aluu	bta3Tii	bitna22ii
	a	ha	khabb**ee**ha	7abb**uwa**	sa2alu**wa**	bta3T**iya**	bitna22**iya**
	un	hun	khabb**ee**hun	7abb**uwun**	sa2alu**wun**	bta3T**iyun**	bitna22**iyun**

11.15 **1** jeebik 3a lmadrase. **3** khabbeehun wara lbeeb. **5** sa2aluu su2aal.
2 le2aana bi lim7aTTa. **4** 7abbuwa li2anna keenit laTiife. **6** bta3Tiik maSaare.

11.16 **1** la ween jeebik? **2** ween le2aana? **3** ween khabbeehun? **4** leesh 7abbuwa? **5** shu sa2aluu? **6** shu bta3Tiik?

ANSWERS & TRANSCRIPTS

11.17		sa7	ghalaT
a	layla 3azamit samiir la 3indun 3a lbeet	x	
b	samiir ma baddo yruu7 la 3ind layla		x
c	samiir baddo ya3rif ween beet layla biZZabT	x	
d	samiir biliff yamiin w yasaar ta yuuSal la 3ind layla		x
e	bas yinzal min lboosTa, biruu7 jeelis	x	
f	beet layla 2abl lmistashfa bi shwayy		x
g	samiir ma 3am bisaddi2 2inno, 2akhiiran, ra7 yitlee2a ma3 3aylit layla	x	
h	samiir, bas mish layla, ra7 ykun mabSuuT		x
i	3eeditlo tleet marraat 2imtiin byije	x	
j	2aalitlo 2inno leezim yije 3a lbisikleet w bi libroteel		x

12.1 1 la tleet tiyyeem.   2 la shakhS waa7ad.   3 baddo takht kbiir / la tneen.
4 li2anno bikuun murii7 2aktar.   5 bi tmeniin dolar.   6 li2anna 2a7san ghirfe w ma3a manZar.

12.2 1 3indkun ghirfe la layle (wi7de), la shakhS waa7ad, fiya takht kbiir/la shakhSeen w 7immeem fi duush, 2iza bitriid$^{\text{le\\o}}$?
2 3indkun ghirfe la 2arba3 layeele, la tleet 2ashkhaaS, fiya tleet tkhuute zghaar w balkoon w manZar, 2iza bitriid$^{\text{le\\o}}$?
3 3indkun ghirfe la saba3 layeele, la khams 2ashkhaaS, fiya takht kbiir w tleete zghaar w talifoon, 2iza bitriid$^{\text{le\\o}}$?
4 3indkun ghirfe la tleet layeele, la shakhSeen, fiya takhteen zghaar w l2internet, ma3 ttirwii2a, 2iza bitriid$^{\text{le\\o}}$?
5 3indkun ghirfe la laylteen, la 2arba3 2ashkhaaS, fiya 2arba3 tkhuute zghaar w 7immem fi baanyo, 2iza bitriid$^{\text{le\\o}}$?
6 3indkun ghirfe la 2usbu3een, la shakhS waa7ad, fiya takht kbiir w balkoon kbiir, 2iza bitriid$^{\text{le\\o}}$?

12.3 1 kam takht?   3 shu bit7ibb$^{\text{e\\o}}$ ykuun fi bi lghirfe?   5 shu bit7ibb$^{\text{e\\o}}$ ykuun fi bi lghirfe?
2 la kam shakhS?   4 la kam layle?   6 la kam shakhS?

12.4 adfecb

12.5	adjective	comparative (more than)	superlative (the most)
	Tawiil^{tall} / 2aSiir^{short}	2aTwal (min^{than}) / 2a2Sar (min)	2aTwal shi / 2a2Sar shi
	naaSi7^{fat} / D3iif ^{skinny}	2anSa7 / 2aD3af	2anSa7 shi / 2aD3af shi
	laTiif / la2iim	2alTaf / 2al2am	2alTaf shi / 2al2am shi

12.6 1 samiir laTiif bas layla 2alTaf. layla 2alTaf minno w min tom. hiyye 2alTaf minnun. layla 2alTaf shi.
2 samiir 7ilo bas layla 2a7la. layla 2a7la minno w min tom. hiyye 2a7la minnun. layla 2a7la shi.
3 samiir ghane bas layla 2aghna. layla 2aghna minno w min tom. hiyye 2aghna minnun. layla 2aghna shi.

12.7 1 badde takht 2akbar, 3mool ma3ruuf.   3 badde manZar 2a7la, ...   5 badde 2arkhaS ghirfe 3indak, ...
2 badde 2internet 2asra3, ...   4 badde 2akbar balkoon, ...   6 2a3raD baanyo 3indik, ...

12.8	Give them to him	3Tii	yyeehun
	Give it^f to me	3Tine	yyeeha
	Give it^m to us	3Tiina	yyee

12.9 1 shu 3imlit? 3aTitkun yyee.   2 shu 3imlit? 7ajazitle yyeeha.   3 shu 3imlit? shtaraalo yyeehun.
4 shu 3imil? Talla3la yyee.   5 shu 3imil? 2akhadla yyeehun.   6 shu 3milto? fata7neelun yyee.

12.10		Sa7	ghalaT
a	layla badda 2ahwe teenye		x
b	samiir leezim yseefir bi shighil	x	
c	layla ra7 tseefir ma3o		x
d	mish ra7 yinzal bi2oteel		x
e	ra7 yi7juz la layla		x
f	baddo yib2a bi l2oteel tleet tiyyeem	x	
g	lghirfe yalle 2akhada fiya takht zghiir		x
h	Talab takht kbiir li2anno bikuun 2arya7 min takht zghiir	x	
i	bi7ibb ma ykuun fi bi lghirfe 7immeem w duush w balkoon		x
j	samiir ra7 yruu7 3a Traablus	x	

13.1 1 bi maT3am   3 3ara2   5 li2anno keen khaayif
2 li2anno ghaale   4 kibbe nayye, tabbuule w mtabbal batinjeen w 7ummuS   6 kees khTuubitun

13.2 1 mu2abbileet,.... 2 Sa7n faleefil,.... 3 7ilo w 2ahwe,.... 4 bas wajbe khafiife,.... 5 shaay biduun sikkar,.... 6 2ahwe biduun 7aliib

13.3 1 ...? tankit fanta, ...   2 ...? 2anniinit biira, ...   3 ...? kees nbiid 2abyaD, ...
4 ...? 2anniinit nbiid 2a7mar, ...   5 ...? kees 3ara2, ...   6 ...? kibbeeyit 3aSiir lbird2aan, ...

13.4 1 ...? Sa7n la7m ba2ar, ...   2 ...? Sa7n la7m khanziir, ...   3 ...? Sa7n samak, ...
4 ...? Sa7n la7m kharuuf, ...   5 ...? Sa7n djeej, ...   6 ...? ma2kuleet ba7riyye, ...

13.5 1 la7m ba2ar mishwe, ...   2 kibbe nayye, ...   3 djeej makhbuuz, ...
4 beeD masluu2, ...   5 yakhnit la7m kharuuf, ...   6 batinjeen mi2le, ...

13.6 1 badc   2 cbad   3 dbac   4 cdba

13.7 1 shu bteekhde? Sa7n batinjeen mi2le.   4 shu byeekhdo? 7ilweyeet w 2ahwe.
2 shu byeekhud? Sa7n samak makhbuuz.   5 shu bteekhud? Sa7n la7m kharuuf mishwe.
3 shu bteekhud? Sa7n djeej 3a rizz.   6 shu bteekhdo? kees nbiid 2abyaD.

13.8 1 2anniine   2 2ann**it** 3aSiir   3 2anniinte   4 2ahwe   5 2ahw**it**a   6 2ahw**it** 2ikhto

13.9 1 liistit l2akl, ...   3 baT7it 3ara2, ...   5 shoorbit samak, ...
2 2anniinit nbiid, ...   4 slaaTit djeej, ...   6 2iT3it ba2leewa, ...

ANSWERS & TRANSCRIPTS

13.10

	ie house b**ee**t my house b**ay**te	string kheeT my string khayTe	oil zeet my oil zayte
our	bayitna	khayiTna	zayitna
your^m	baytak	khayTak	zaytak
their	baytun	khayTun	zaytun

13.11 1 teaches/makes learn 3 scared/made scared 5 get you to listen to
2 gave her to drink / got her to drink 4 polished/made shine 6 makes you work

13.12	say	said	tell/speak	told/spoke 7kiit
2ana	b2uul	2ilt	bi7ke	7kiit
ni7na	min2uul	2ilna	mni7ke	7kiina
2inta	bit2uul	2ilt	bti7ke	7kiit
2inte	bit2uule	2ilte	bti7ke	7kiite
2into	bit2uulo	2ilto	bti7ko	7kiito
huwwe	bi2uul	2aal	byi7ke	7ike
hiyye	bit2uul	2aalit	bti7ke	7ikyit
hinne	bi2uulo	2aalo	byi7ko	7ikyo

13.13 1 shu 2aal? 2 shu 3am bit2uule? 3 shu 2aalit? 4 shu 7ike? 5 shu 3am yi7ko? 6 shu 7kiit?

13.14		Sa7	ghalaT
a	lmaT3am ktiir rkhiiS 3a samiir		x
b	samiir byiTlub liistit l2akl ma3 liistit lmashruub	x	
c	samiir jeeb layla 3a hayda lmaT3am ta y2illa shi muhimm	x	
d	byiTilbo 2anniinit nbiid 2abyaD		x
e	lgarsoon bijiblun tleet keseet		x
f	samiir ma Talab 2illa Sa7n waa7ad ba3d lmeeza		x
g	layla bit2uul la samiir 2inno leezim ykhaaf w ma y2illa shi		x
h	layla badda 2inno samiir yfahhima leesh jeeba 3a ha lmaT3am	x	
i	samiir baddo yishrab ma3 layla kees khTuubitun	x	
j	2iza 2aalit layla 'la2' samiir ra7 y2uum w yimshe	x	

14.1 1 yoom ssabt 2 ssee3a tmeene 3 ra7 yruu7o yitrawwa2o mne2iish 4 ra7 yruu7o 3a lmool
5 l2amiiS w lbanTaloon w SSibbaaT yalle 2aalit la samiir 2inna 7abbittun 6 ghaale
14.2 1 la ween raayi7? 2 la ween ray7iin? 3 la ween raay7a? 4 la ween ray7iin?
14.3 1 raayi7 3a lmool. 2 ray7iin 3a ssuu2. 3 raay7a 3a ssupermaarket. 4 ray7iin 3a ddikkeen.
14.4 1 shu badda tishitre? 3 shu baddik tishitre? 5 shu badde 2ishitre?
2 shu baddun yishitro? 4 shu baddkun tishitro? 6 shu baddna nishitre?
14.5 1 ... bakeet zibde. 2 ... loo7 Sabuun. 3 ... kiilo ba2leewa. 4 ... kiis rizz. 5 ... ma3juun sneen. 6 ... 2iT3it jibne.
14.6 1 ra7 yjarrib lkanze lkhaDra. 3 ra7 jarrib lbanTaloon lbinne. 5 ra7 jarrib SSibbaaT l2aswad.
2 ra7 yjarrbo lkalseet lbiiD. 4 ra7 njarrib lfisTaan l2azra2. 6 ra7 njarrib shshoort l2aSfar.
14.7 1 naa2So nishsheefe. 2 naa2iSna ghisseele. 3 naa2iSun birraad. 4 naa2iSne maaycroweyv.
14.8 1 baddo yjiib karaase. 2 baddna njiib tkhuute. 3 baddna njiib mobaayl. 4 badde jiib kanabeyeet. 5 badde jiib talfizyoon.
14.9 1 shu shtara? shtara kirse. 3 shu shtarayt? shtarayt mreyeet. 5 2addeesh dafa3t 3a lkirse? dafa3t khamsiin dolar.
2 shu shtarayto? shtarayna takht. 4 shu shtaro? shtaro kiilo tiffee7. 6 2addeesh dafa3te 3a ttakht? dafa3t miit dolar.
14.10 1 2addeesh kallafito? kallafito tisa3 dolaraat. 4 2addeesh kallafita? kallafita tleetaw 2arb3iin dolar.
2 2addeesh kallafa? kallafa dolareen. 5 2addeesh kallafitna? kallafitna 3ishriin dolar.
3 2addeesh kallafitne? kallafitne tleetaw sab3iin dolar. 6 2addeesh kallafitun? kallafitun tis3iin dolar.
14.11 1 2amiiS 2 khzeene 3 SibbaaT 4 bi2ra 5 mishwe 6 mobaayl
14.13 1 shu jeebitla? 2 shu btekhdiilun? 3 shu rakhkhaSneela? 4 shu 7kitillo? 5 shu bi2raalun? 6 bi shu sama7uulo?

14.14

CARDINAL		ORDINAL						
1	waa7ad	1st	2awwal/2awwle	11th	li7da3sh			
2	tneen	2nd	teene/teenye	12th	ttna3sh	20th	l3ishriin	21st	lwa7daw 3ishriin
3	tleete	3rd	teelit/teelte	13th	ttleetta3sh	30th	ttletiin	32nd	ttneenaw tletiin
4	2arb3a	4th	raabi3/raab3a	14th	l2arba3ta3sh	40th	l2arb3iin	43rd	ttleetaw 2arb3iin
5	khamse	5th	khaamis/khaamse	15th	lkhamsta3sh	50th	lkhamsiin	54th	l2arb3aw khamsiin
6	sitte	6th	seedis/seedse	16th	ssitta3sh	60th	ssittiin	65th	lkhamsaw sittiin
7	sab3a	7th	seebi3/seeb3a	17th	ssaba3ta3sh	70th	ssab3iin	76th	ssittaw sab3iin
8	tmeene	8th	teemin/teemne	18th	ttmeenta3sh	80th	ttmeniin	87th	ssab3aw tmeniin
9	tis3a	9th	teesi3/tees3a	19th	ttisa3ta3sh	90th	ttis3iin	98th	ttmeenaw tis3iin
10	3ashra	10th	3aashir/3aashra					100th	lmiyye

14.15 1 bi zzikra tteelte 3 bi zzikra ttna3sh 5 bi zzikra lmiyye w khamsiin
2 bi zzikra sseeb3a 4 bi zzikra lwa7daw tletiin

ANSWERS & TRANSCRIPTS

14.16

		Sa7	ghalaT
a	ra7 yitlee2o yoom l2a7ad		x
b	byishitro kill shi w byirja3o bi lleel		x
c	layla bit2uul 2inno 2ahla mle3iin		x
d	layla btinzal bas samiir yZammir	x	
e	samiir Saar min 3aylit layla	x	
f	2awwal shi biruu7o 3a ssuuppermarket		x
g	byitrawwa2o mne2iish	x	
h	layla badda tishitriilo SSibbaaT yalle huwwe 7abbo		x
i	lkhaatim yalle shtaraala yyee rkhiiS		x
j	ma ra7 yi2idro yishitro beet 2ariiban	x	

15.1 1 lamma bikuun romantiike ma3a
2 baddo ya3rif kill l2ishya yalle bit7ibba w ma bit7ibba.
3 baddo ya3rif 2iza mseefra shi marra 3a lkheerij.
4 li2anno 2eekil w sheerib ktiir.
5 2e, ma 3ada lfaTbool.
6 wleedun

15.2 1 shu hiweeyitun? 3 shu hiweeyita 5 shu hiweeytik?
2 shu hiweeyitkun 4 shu hiweeyto? 6 shu hiweeyitna?

15.3 1 bi7ibbo li3b lwara2 w shshighil bi lijnayne.   4 bi7ibb li3b lmusii2a w rrasm.
2 min7ibb nit3allam 3arabe w li3b rryaDa.   5 b7ibb shshighil bi lijnayne w rrasm.
3 bit7ibb titsamma3 3a lmusii2a w ssafar.   6 min7ibb Seed ssamak w ssinama.

15.4 1 bi7ibbo li3b lwara2 bas ma bi7ibbo shshighil bi lijnayne.   4 bi7ibb li3b lmusii2a bas ma bi7ibb rrasm.
2 min7ibb nit3allam 3arabe bas ma min7ibb li3b rryaDa.   5 b7ibb shshighil bi lijnayne bas ma b7ibb rrasm.
3 bit7ibb titsamma3 3a lmusii2a bas ma bit7ibb ssafar.   6 min7ibb Seed ssamak bas ma min7ibb ssinama.

15.6 1 bi7ibb l2afleem lwasee2iQiyye.   3 b7ibb 2afleem rri3b.   5 min7ibb 2afleem ddraama.
2 bi7ibbo 2afleem lmughaamara.   4 bit7ibb l2afleem yalle bit7azzin.   6 min7ibb l2afleem lbulisiyye.

15.8 1 2inte seekne bi London.   3 hiyye ni3seene ktiir.   5 ni7na nezliin bi l2oteel la tleet 2asabii3.
2 halla2 hinne 2e3diin bi SSaff.   4 2into msefriin 3a lyabaan.   6 2inta seemi3 2inno libraziil balad 7ilo.

15.9 1 ween seekne?   3 2addeesh ni3seene?   5 2addeesh be2yiin bi l2oteel?
2 ween 2e3diin halla2?   4 la ween msefriin?   6 shu seemi3?

15.11

1 living
a huwwe seekin bi beriiz
b ssine lmaaDye keen seekin bi london
c ssine ljeey ra7 ykuun seekin bi sidni

2 sitting
a halla2 2ana 2ee3id bi SSaff
b l2usbuu3 lmaaDe bi ha lwa2t kint 2ee3id bi SSaff
c l2usbuu3 ljeey bi ha lwa2t bkuun 2ee3id bi SSaff

3 sleepy
a ni7na halla2 mish ktiir ni3seniin
b mbeeri7 ssee3a 7da3sh bi lleel kinna ktiir ni3seniin
c bukra ba3d ssee3a 7da3sh bi lleel minkuun ktiir ni3seniin

4 paid
a ma yhimmik^{don't worry}, 2ana deefi3 lfetuura
b kint deefi3 lfetuura lamma 2ijit layla ta tidfa3a
c bukra 2abl ma shuufa, bkuun deefi3 lfetuura

15.12

		PRESENT			PAST		
	Active	Passive		Active		Passive	
	I injure	verb	adjective	I injured	verb	adjective	
		I get injured	I am injured		I got injured	I was injured	
		bin.i.i.	ma..uu.		n.a.a.	kint ma..uu.	
2ana	bijra7	binjiri7	majruu7 majruu7a majru7iin	jara7t	njara7t	kint	majruu7 majruu7a majru7iin
ni7na	mnijra7	mninjiri7		jara7na	njara7na	kinna	
2inta	btijra7	btinjiri7		jara7t	njara7t	kint	
2inte	btijra7e	btinjir7e		jara7te	njara7te	kinte	
2into	btijra7o	btinjir7o		jara7to	njara7to	kinto	
huwwe	byijra7	byinjiri7		jara7	njara7	keen	
hiyye	btijra7	btinjiri7		jara7it	njara7it	keenit	
hinne	byijra7o	byinjir7o		jara7o	njara7o	keeno	

15.13 **Present:**   **Past:**

1	2ana	bisru2	binsiri2	masruu2	sara2t	nsara2t	kint masruu2
2	hiyye	btiksur	btinkisir	maksuura	kasarit	nkasarit	keenit maksuura
3	2ana^f	bib3at	binbi3it	mab3uute	ba3att	nba3att	kint mab3uute
4	huwwe	byil3am	byinli3ib	mal3uub	li3ib	nla3am	keen mal3uub
5	ni7na	mnib3at	mninbi3it	mab3utiin	ba3atna	nba3atna	kinna mab3utiin
6	hinne	byishrabo	byinshirbo	mashruubiin	shirbo	nsharabo	keeno mashrubiin

15.14 1 ma bishrab 2ahwe 2abilma neem.   4 mneekhud kalibna ma3na weenma minruu7.
2 byeekul ba3idma yirja3 3a lbeet.   5 birtee7 lamma bkuun ti3been.
3 killma bitseefir btinsiri2.   6 bneem killma bkuun ni3seene.

ANSWERS & TRANSCRIPTS

15.15			Sa7	ghalaT
	a	samiir baddo ya3rif shu layla bit7ibb ta3mul bi wa2t lfaraagh	x	
	b	layla bit7ibb samiir 2aktar shi lamma ma bikuun romantiike ma3a	x	
	c	layla ma bit7ibb truu7 tishitre 2ishya; bas bit7ibb lfaTbool		x
	d	layla mseefra ktiir marraat 3a lkheerij		x
	e	samiir ba3d mish 2eekil wala[nor] sheerib lyoom		x
	f	layla bitfaDDil tib2a bi lbeet w ma tshuuf 2aSdiQaa2a		x
	g	layla w samiir bi7ibbo nafs l2ishya		x
	h	ra7 y2aDDo 2iyyeem 7ilwe sawa	x	
	i	ma bi7ibbo yeekhdo wleedun ma3un lamma biseefro		x
	j	killun ra7 yinbiSto sawa	x	

16.1 1 bi libneen. 2 ba3d l3aaSme, bayruut. 3 TTa2s ktiir 7ilo w mishmis.
4 bukra, li2anno TTa2s ra7 ykuun 3aaTil. ra7 ykuun fi shite w hawa. 2afDal 2inno ma ykuuno barra.
5 fi jeemi3 kbiir.   6 l3aalam killo.

16.2 1 ... 3a lma3aalim.   2 ... 3a lkaneeyis w ljaweemi3.   3 ... 3a lmawee2i3 tterikhiyye / l2asaraat l2adiime.
4 ... 3a lmabeene tturasiyye.   5 ... 3a lmat7af lfanne.   6 ... 3a lma3raD.

16.3 1 fi bard   2 3am titluj   3 fi hawa   4 3am bitshatte   5 fi shoob   6 TTa2s mghayyim

16.4

ktb	l3b	3ml	Tbkh	khbz	Srf	3lm	mrD	Swr
writing	*playing*	*doing*	*cooking*	*baking*	*spending*	*knowledge*	*illness*	*photographing*
maktuub	mal3uub	ma3muul	maTbuukh	makhbuuz	maSruuf	ma3luum	mamruuD	
written	*played*	*done/made*	*cooked*	*baked*	*spent*	*known*	*diseased*	

16.5 **(a)** 1 skn 2 Tyr 3 fnn 4 2rb 5 Tbkh 6 mrn
(b) 1 The resident resides in a residence.
2 The pilot flies the plane from the airport.
3 The artist likes art and creates works of art.
4 When my relative bought a house and got closer, he ended up living very close to me.
5 The cook likes cooking and cooks a lot in the kitchen.
6 These exercises train you to speak Arabic.

16.6 1 law bitzuurne, kint bzuurak   2 law ziritne, kint zirtak   3 2iza bitzuurne, bzuurak
4 2iza btishrab, bishrab   5 law shribt, kint shribt   6 law btishrab, kint bishrab

16.7 1 You don't like art = Is not happening.   2 We may go out = May happen.   3 You/she may like arak = May happen.
4 You didn't eat enough = Didn't happen.   5 You may come with me = May happen. 6 She didn't drink = Didn't happen.

16.8 1 bti3izmo   2 byiskaro   3 sa2alo   4 mnirja3   5 btit3allame   6 shift

16.9

			Sa7	ghalaT
	a	layla w samiir ra7 ySiiro siwwee7	x	
	b	baddun yshuufo lkheerij 2abilma yshuufo libneen		x
	c	baddun yshuufo libneen 2abilma yshuufo lkheerij	x	
	d	ra7 yballsho bi lmat7af lwaTane	x	
	e	ra7 yruu7o 3a lmat7af lamma bikuun TTa2s 3aaTil	x	
	f	ra7 ykuuno barra lamma bikuun fi shite w hawa		x
	g	lkatidraa2iyye b3iide 3an ljeemi3		x
	h	ra7 yruu7o 3a lmat7af lfanne ta yshuufo law7aat picaasso	x	
	i	2awwal shi, baddun ytalifno ta ya3irfo 2aw2aat fat7 lmat7af	x	
	j	ra7 yshuufo l3aalam ba3idma yshuufo libneen	x	

APPENDIX 1

QUESTION WORDS   kiif mnis2al

Question word		Example
How	kiif	kiifak / kiif 7aalak? [How are you?]
How long/big	2addeesh	2addeesh b2iit bi l2oteel? [How long did you stay at the hotel?] 2addeesh kibr lghirfe? [How big is the room?]
How many	kam	kam shakhS? [How many people?]
How much	b2addeesh	b2addeesh kiilo ttiffee7? [How much is a kilo of apples?]
What [involving numbers]	b2addeesh	b2addeesh shshahr lyoom? [What's the date today?]
What	shu	shu 2ismak? [What's your name?] shu 3am ta3mul? [What are you doing?]
When	2imtiin	2imtiin 3iid mileedak? [When is your birthday?]
Where	ween	ween seekin? [Where do you live?]
Where from	min ween	2inta min ween? [Where are you from?]
Where to	la ween	la ween raayi7? [Where are you going?]
Which	2ayya	ni7na bi 2ayya faSl? [Which season are we in?]
Who	miin	miin hayda? [Who is this?]
Why	leesh	leesh 3am tit3allam 3arabe? [Why are you learning Arabic?]

PREPOSITIONS   7arf jarr

about	3an
as	ka
at	3ind
despite	raghm
in	bi
of/from	min

on	3ala
since	min
to/for	la$^{+nn/vb}$/ta^{+vb}
until	7atta
with	ma3

CONJUNTIONS   7arf 3aTf

and	w
as	bima 2inno
because	li2anno
but	bas
unless	2illa 2iza
while	lamma

APPENDIX 2
PRESENT TENSE

LEARN THE MODEL VERBS BY HEART.

MODEL bzuur — If the **prefix is in a consonant cluster,** apply the consonant cluster rule [Count two consonants from the back and insert i]

PERSON	visit			be			see			go		
	prefix	Stem	Suffix									
1st 2ana	b			b			b			b		
ni7na	min			min			min			min		
2nd 2inta	bit			bit			bit			bit		
2inte	bit	zuur	e	bit	kuun	e	bit	shuuf	e	bit	ruu7	e
2into	bit		o	bit		o	bit		o	bit		o
3rd huwwe	bi			bi			bi			bi		
hiyye	bit			bit			bit			bit		
hinne	bi		o	bi		o	bi		o	bi		o

MODEL bil3ab — If 1st person **b is followed by a vowel,** insert **y** between them in the 3rd person [except for hiyye]

PERSON	play			drink			swim			pay		
	prefix	Stem	Suffix									
1st 2ana	bi			bi			bi			bi		
ni7na	mni			mni			mni			mni		
2nd 2inta	bti			bti			bti			bti		
2inte	bti	l3am	e	bti	shrab	e	bti	sba7	e	bti	dfa3	e
2into	bti		o	bti		o	bti		o	bti		o
3rd huwwe	byi			byi			byi			byi		
hiyye	bti			bti			bti			bti		
hinne	byi		o	byi		o	byi		o	byi		o

MODEL bitmashsha — If the **stem ends in a vowel,** drop this end vowel when you add a suffix [e/o].

PERSON	stroll			read			buy			give			throw		
	prefix	Stem	Suffix												
1st 2ana	bi	tmashsha		bi	2ra		b	ishitre		b	a3Te		bi	rme	
ni7na	mni	tmashsha		mni	2ra		mn	ishitre		mn	a3Te		mni	rme	
2nd 2inta	bti	tmashsha		bti	2ra		bt	ishitre		bt	a3Te		bti	rme	
2inte	bti	tmashsh	e	bti	2r	e	bt	ishitr	e	bt	a3T	e	bti	rm	e
2into	bti	tmashsh	o	bti	2r	o	bt	ishitr	o	bt	a3T	o	bti	rm	o
3rd huwwe	byi	tmashsha		byi	2ra		by	ishitre		by	a3Te		byi	rme	
hiyye	bti	tmashsha		bti	2ra		bt	ishitre		bt	a3Te		bti	rme	
hinne	byi	tmashsh	o	byi	2r	o	by	ishitr	o	by	a3T	o	byi	rm	o

MODEL ba3mul — If the **stem ends in a consonant** -drop its last short vowel **i/u** [not a] when a suffix is added.
-then apply the consonant cluster rule if need be.

PERSON	do			eat			travel			drink			hear		
	prefix	Stem	Suffix												
1st 2ana	b	a3mul		b	eekul		b	seefir		bi	shrab		bi	sma3	
ni7na	mn	a3mul		mn	eekul		min	seefir		mni	shrab		mni	sma3	
2nd 2inta	bt	a3mul		bt	eekul		bit	seefir		bti	shrab		bti	sma3	
2inte	bt	a3iml	e	bt	eekl	e	bit	seefr	e	bti	shrab	e	bti	sma3	e
2into	bt	a3iml	o	bt	eekl	o	bit	seefr	o	bti	shrab	o	bti	sma3	o
3rd huwwe	by	a3mul		by	eekul		bi	seefir		byi	shrab		byi	sma3	
hiyye	bt	a3mul		bt	eekul		bit	seefir		bti	shrab		bti	sma3	
hinne	by	a3iml	o	by	eekl	o	bi	seefr	o	byi	shrab	o	byi	sma3	o

PAST TENSE

MODEL 2akalt — If the verb is **REGULAR** Stem stays the same throughout

PERSON		ate		contacted		helped		swam		travelled		worked	
1st 2ana			t		t		t		t		t		t
ni7na			na		na		na		na		na		na
2nd 2inta			t		t		t		t		t		t
2inte	2akal		te	ttaSal	te	see3ad	te	saba7	te	seefar	te	shtaghal	te
2into			to		to		to		to		to		to
3rd huwwe													
hiyye			it		it		it		it		it		it
hinne			o		o		o		o		o		o

If the verb is **IRREGULAR** Stem changes in the 3rd person

MODELS tmashshayt — 2riit

PERSON	If 1st person has **ay**, y/ay disappear in the 3rd person.						If 1st person has a **long ii**, in the 3rd person: insert **i** in the 1st syllable and **e/y** at the stem end						
	strolled			bought			read			stayed		told		cried
1st 2ana			t			t			t		t		t	t
ni7na			na			na			na		na		na	na
2nd 2inta	tmashshay		t	shtaray		t	2rii		t	b2ii	t	7kii	t	bkii t
2inte			te			te			te		te		te	te
2into			to			to			to		to		to	to
3rd huwwe	tmashsha			shtara			**2ire**			bi2e		7ike		bike
hiyye	tmashsh		it	shtar		it	**2iry**		it	bi2y	it	7iky	it	biky it
hinne	tmashsh		o	shtar		o	**2iry**		o	bi2y	o	7iky	o	biky o

MODEL 3milt ³ᵐˡ If the verb has a **short i** and a **3-consonant root**, another **i** is inserted after the first letter in the 3rd person.

PERSON	did		drank		played		heard		grew (up)		regretted	
1st 2ana		t		t		t		t		t		t
ni7na		na		na		na		na		na		na
2nd 2inta	3mil	t	shrib	t	l3ib	t	smi3	t	kbir	t	ndim	t
2inte		te		te		te		te		te		te
2into		to		to		to		to		to		to
3rd huwwe	3imil		shirib		li3ib		simi3		kibir		nidim	
hiyye	3iml	it	shirb	it	li3b	it	sim3	it	kibr	it	nidm	it
hinne	3iml	o	shirb	o	li3b	o	sim3	o	kibr	o	nidm	o

MODEL kint ᵏⁿ If the verb has a **short i** and a **2-consonant root**, **i** turns into a long **ee/aa** if guttural/ending has **r** in the 3rd person.

PERSON	was		sold		slept		visited		said		fear	
1st 2ana		t		t		t		t		t		t
ni7na		na		na		na		na		na		na
2nd 2inta	kin	t	bi3	t	nim	t	zir	t	ri7	t	khif	t
2inte		te		te		te		te		te		te
2into		to		to		to		to		to		to
3rd huwwe	keen		bee3		neem		zaar		raa7		khaaf	
hiyye	keen	it	bee3	it	neem	it	zaar	it	raa7	it	khaaf	it
hinne	keen	o	bee3	o	neem	o	zaar	o	raa7	o	khaaf	o

ADDING PRONOMINAL SUFFIXES to show the object of the action.

MODELS: bishuuf — 3aTa — 7abbo — bya3Te

If verb ends in a consonant:			If verb ends in a vowel: make the short vowel long and start the suffix with a consonant.										
			a becomes **aa** 3rd person **aah**				**o** becomes **uu** 3rd person **uw**				**e** becomes **ii** 3rd person **iy**		
bishuuf he sees ...		sim3it she heard ...	3aTa he gave ...		lee2a he met ...		7abbo they liked ...		sa2alo they asked ...		bya3Te he gives ...		byije I receive ...
	ne ᵐᵉ	ne	ne		ne		ne		ne		ne		ne
	na ᵘˢ	na	na		na		na		na		na		na
	ak ʸᵒᵘ ᵐ	ak	k	7abbuu	k	sa2aluu	k	bya3Tii	k	byijii	k
bi shuuf	ik ʸᵒᵘ ᶠ	sim3it ik	3aTaa ke	le2aa	ke		ke		ke		ke		ke
	kun ʸᵒᵘ ᵖ	kun	kun		kun		kun		kun		kun		kun
	o ʰⁱᵐ	o					7abbuu		sa2aluu		bya3Tii		byijii
	a ʰᵉʳ	a	ha		ha		7abbu wa		sa2alu wa		bya3Ti ya		byiji ya
	un ᵘˢ	un	hun		hun		7abbu wun		sa2alu wun		bya3Ti yun		byiji yun

APPENDIX 3

VERB TENSE COMPARISON

PAST	PRESENT	FUTURE
I ate (ma) 2akalt	I eat (ma) beekul	I will eat (ma/mish) ra7 2eekul
I was eating (ma) kint 3am beekul	I am eating (ma/mish) 3am beekul	I am going to / I will be eating (ma/mish) ra7 kuun / (ma) bkuun 3am beekul
I had eaten (ma) kint 2eekil	I have eaten (mish) 2eekil	I am going to / I will have eaten (ma/mish) ra7 kuun / (ma) bkuun 2eekil
I might have eaten yimkin (ma) kint 2eekil	I may eat yimkin (ma) 2eekul	I may eat tomorrow yimkin (ma) 2eekul bukra
I had a book (ma) keen 3inde kteeb	I have a book (ma) 3inde kteeb	I am going to / I will have a book (ma/mish) ra7 ykuun / (ma) bikuun 3inde kteeb

GLOSSARY: LEBANESE - ENGLISH

GLOSSARY

LEBANESE	ENGLISH
2a7mar ^{7amra\7umr}	red
2aab	August
2ab ^{aweet}	father
2abadan	at all
2abilma ^{+vb}	before
2abl	before/in advance
2abyaD ^{bayDa\biiD}	white
2adaar	March
2addeesh ^{ssee3a/lmaseefe}?	how much^{time/distance}?
2adiim ^{2deem}	old
2afDal	better
2ahlan	hello/welcome/pleased to meet you
2ahwe ^{2aheewe}	coffee/cafe
2akh ^{2ikhwe}	brother
2akhDar ^{khaDra\khiDr}	green
2akhiiran	finally
2akl ^{ma2kuleet}	food
2alam ^{2leem}	pen
2alam rSaaS	pencil
2alf ^{2lufeet}	thousand
2aliil ^{2leel}	little
2almaane	German
2almaanya	Germany
2amar ^{2maar}	moon
2ameerka	America
2amerkeene ^{iyye}	American
2amiiS ^{2imSaan}	shirt
2ana	I (am)
2anniine ^{2aneene}	bottle
2arb3a	four
2ariib ^{2raab} (min)	close (to)
2ariib ^{2raayib}	relative^{family}
2ariiban	soon
2asaraat	ruins
2asaraat 2adiime	ancient ruins
2aSfar ^{Safra\Sifr}	yellow
2aSiir ^{2Saar}	short
2aSl	origin^{country of}
2aswad ^{sawda\suud}	black
2aw	or
2awe ^{2weeya}	strong
2awwal shi	first| thing/of all
2awwilt mbeeri7	day before yesterday
2ayluul	September
2ayya? ^{in a question}	which?
2ayyaar	May
2azra2 ^{zar2a\zir2}	blue
2e	yes^{familiar}
2eekhir ⁱⁱⁿ	last
2elektroniyyeet	electronics
2espaanya	Spain
2iddeem	in front of / across the road from
2ihtimeem	concern
2ikht ^{2ikhweet}	sister
2illa ^{time}	to/minus
2imm ^{eet}	mother
2imtiin?	when?^{in a question}
2ingliteerra	England
2ingliize ^{2ingliiz}	English
2inne ^{na/ak...}	to^{after verb eg I wanted to}
2inno	that
2inta	you^m
2inte	you^f
2internet	internet
2intibeeh	attention
2into	you^p
2irlanda	Ireland
2irlande ^{iyye}	Irish
2ishya ma3ruuDa	exhibits
2ism ^{2aseeme}	name
2iSSa 2aSiire	short story
2iSSa ^{2iSSaS}	story
2isteez ^{2aseetze}	teacher/sir
2iT3a ^{2iTa3}	piece
2iT3it 7ilo	piece of cake
2iTaalya	Italy
2iza	if
2iza bitriid	please^{if you}
2orooppa	Europe
2ostraale ^{iyye}	Australian
2ostraalya	Australia
2otobiis ^{eet}	bus
2usbuu3 ^{2asabii3}	week
3a mihlak	slowly
3a/3ala	on
3am ^{prefix equivalent to verb+ing suffix in English}	...ing
3aadatan	usually
3afwan ^{inv.}	welcome^{response to shukran} /excuse me
3ala raa7tak	at your leisure/as you please
3aalam	world
3amal ^{2a3meel} fanne^{iyye}	work of art
3aamm	general^{adj}
3ara2	arak^{traditional alcoholic drink: aniseed based, diluted with water}
3arabe	Arabic
3arD ^{3ruuD}	exhibit
3aaSfe ^{3awaaSif}	storm
3asha	dinner
3ashra	ten
3aSiir	juice
3aaSme ^{3awaaSim}	capital
3atii2 ^{3tee2}	old
3aaTil ⁱⁱⁿ	bad
3atm	darkness
3ayb	shame(ful)
3ayle ^{3iyal}	family
3aziime ^{3azeeyim}	invitation
3ibaara ^{at}	expression/phrase
3iid mileed	birthday
3imle ^{at}	currency
3ind layla	at Layla's
3indak	have^{you}
3inween ^{3anawiin}	address
3iTle ^{et}	holiday
3mool ma3ruuf	please^{if you}
7abiibe ^{ete}	dear^{my} /love^{my}
7abl ^{7beel}	rope

GLOSSARY: LEBANESE - ENGLISH

Lebanese	English
7adas [2a7dees]	action/event
7add	next to/near
7adii2a [7adeeyi2]	garden/park
7aaDir [iin]	present/ready
7aaDir [inv.]	sure [response to person being served]
7aDirtak [ik/kun]	you [respectful]
7akiim [7ukama]	doctor
7all [7luul]	solution
7araam!	poor thing!
7arf 3aTf	conjunction [and/but/or ...]
7arf [7ruuf]	letter [of alphabet]
7arf jarr	preposition [in/on/at ...]
7arf mit7arrik	vowel
7arf seekin	consonant
7atta	till/so that/even
7awla/7aweele	around
7aziin [iin]	sad
7illaa2 [iin]	hairdresser
7ilo [7ilwe\iin]	beautiful/nice/interesting
7ilo [7ilweyeet]	cake// dessert
7immeem [eet]	bathroom/toilet
7izn [2a7zeen]	sadness
7ummuS	chickpeas /sesame seed paste dip
7zayraan	June
b2aDDe [2aDDayt]	spend [time]
b2addesh?	how much [cost]?
b2uul [2ilt]	say
b2uum [2imt]	get up [out of bed]
b3ambe [3ambayt]	fill in
b3ayyiT [3ayyaTt] la	call out to
b3iid [3idt]	repeat
b3iid [b3aad] (3an)	far (from)
b7ibb [7abbayt]	like/love
ba2a	anymore/so
ba2leewa	baklava
ba3d	yet/till/after
ba3d bukra	day after tomorrow
ba3d i DDohr	afternoon (in the)
ba3d [tleet sniin]	in [three years]
ba3deen	afterwards
ba3idma [+vb]	after
ba3mul [3milt]	do
ba3rif [3rift]	know
ba3Te [3aTayt/3Tiit]	give
ba7r [b7uur]	sea
badde [keen badde]	want [wanted]
bakhiil [bukhala]	stingy
bakkiir	early
bala	without
bala maSkhara	don't muck around/mock
balad [bleed/bildeen]	country
barke/balke	maybe
balkoon [blekiin]	balcony
banTaloon [bnaTliin]	pants
baanyo	bath(tub)
bard	cold
barra	outside
bas	but/just
baaS [eet]	bus
baT7a [at]	flask
baTii2 [iin]	slow
batinjeen	eggplant
bayy [eet]	father
bballish [ballasht]	start
bDayyi3 [Dayya3t]	waste/lose
bee2e	remainder/rest/change [money]
bee2e [yiin]	staying
beeb [bweeb]	door
beekhud [2akhadt]	take
beekhud maw3id	make an appointment
beekul [2akalt]	eat
been	between
been 2oSeen	brackets [in]
beet [byuut]	house
bfaDDil [faDDalt]	prefer
bfii2 [fi2t]	wake up
bfuut [fitt]	enter
bi	in
bi l3aks	on the contrary
bi sir3a	quickly
bi [tleete 2aab]	on [the third of August]
bi23ud [2a3adt]	stay [in a city/hotel] // sit down
bi2dir [2dirt]	can/able to
bi2ra [2riit]	read
bi2Ta3 [2aTa3t]	cross [street]
bi3ra2 [3ri2t]	perspire
bi3tizir [3tazart]	sorry
bi3zum [3azamt]	invite
bi7Dar [7Dirt]	see [film]
bi7juz [7ajazt]	book [trip]
bi7ke [7kiit]	speak/tell
bi7kum [7akamt]	dictate/give orders
bib2a [b2iit]	stay [in a city/hotel]
bib3at [ba3att]	send
bideeye [et]	beginning
bidfa3 [dafa3t]	pay
biDhar [Dahart]	go out
biduun	without
bifham [fhimt]	understand
bifta7 [fata7t]	open
biftikir [ftakart]	think
bighfa [ghfiit]	fall asleep
bighiTT [ghaTT] 3a 2albe	faint [lose consciousness]
bije [jiit]	come
bijra7 [jara7t]	injure/wound
bikaffe [kaffa]	enough
bikallif [kallaf]	cost [(it) vb]
bikhdum [khadamt]	serve/be of service
bikhlaS [khalaSt]	finish
biksur [kasart]	break
biktishif [ktashaft]	discover
biktub [katabt]	write
bikzub [kazabt]	lie [be dishonest]
bil3ab [l3ibt]	play
bilbus [lbist]	wear
bilhe [lahayt/lhiit]	distract
bimshe [mshiit]	walk
bin2ul [na2alt]	move house

GLOSSARY: LEBANESE - ENGLISH

Lebanese	English
bin3as [n3ist]	sleepy
binball [nballayt]	get wet
binbiSit [nbaSatt]	have a good time
bindam [ndimt]	regret
bineesib [neesab]	suit [vb]
binne [binniyye]	brown
binsa [nsiit]	forget
binsiri2 [nsara2t]	robbed [get]
bint [baneet]	girl
binti2id [nta2adt]	criticise
bintibih [ntabaht]	pay attention
binTur [naTart]	wait
binzal [nzilt]	get off [bus] / stay [in hotel]
binzirib [nzarabt]	stuck [be, in a place]
biira	beer
bird2aane [bird2aan]	orange
birja3 [rji3t]	return
birnayTa [braniiT]	hat
birraad [eet]	fridge
birsum [rasamt]	draw [picture]
birtee7 [rta7t]	rest/relax
bis2al [sa2alt]	ask
bisba7 [saba7t]	swim
bishba3 [shbi3t]	full [be, of food]
bishfa [shfiit]	recover [health]
bishi3 [iin]	ugly
bishitre [shtarayt/shtriit]	buy
bishkur [shakart]	thank
bishrab [shribt]	drink
bishrab [shribt] kees	toast [in celebration]
bishtighil [shtaghalt]	work
bisikleet [eet]	bicycle
biskar [skirt]	get drunk
biskut [sakatt]	silent [be]
bisma3 [smi3t]	hear
bismarr [smarrayt]	tan
bisru2 [sara2t]	steal
biSruf [Saraft]	spend [money]
bit3allam [t3allamt]	learn
bit7addas [t7addast]	converse
bitba3 [taba3t]	follow
biTbukh [Tabakht]	cook
bitdammi3 [dammai3t] 3ayne	become tearful
bitfarraj [tfarrajt] 3a	watch [TV]
bitjawwaz [tjawwazt]	get married
bitlee2a [tlee2ayt]	meet up
biTlub [Talabt]	order [drink/food]
bitmashsha [tmashshayt]	go for a walk
bitrawwa2 [trawwa2t]	have breakfast
bitriid [e\o?]	would you like? [used by person offering service]
bitruk [tarakt]	leave
biTrush [Tarasht]	paint [eg house]
bitsamma3 [tsamma3t]	listen
bitsee2al [tsee2alt]	wonder
bitshatte 3a lkhafiif	drizzle
bitshatte [shattit]	rain [vb]
bitTalla3 [TTalla3t]	look
bittiSil [ttaSalt]	contact
bitzallaj [tzallajt]	ski/skate
biw2af [w2ift]	stop/stand
biZZabt	exactly
bjarrib [jarrabt]	try on
bjiib [jibt]	bring
bkammil [kammalt]	complete
bkhabbe [khabbayt]	hide
bkhaaf [khift]	worry/be afraid
bkhaaTrak [ik/kun]	bye [person leaving]
bkhaTTit [khaTTat]	plan
bkhawwif [khawwaft]	scare
bkuun [kint]	be [was]
blammi3 [lamma3t]	polish [shoes]
bliff [laffayt]	turn
bmuut bi heek shi	I adore that sort of thing
bna22e [na22ayt/bikhtaar khtart]	choose
bneem [nimt]	sleep
booSTa [at]	bus
brakhkhe [rakhkhayt]	loosen
broteel [eet]	singlet
bruu7 [ri7t] 3a	go to
bruu7 [ri7t] ra7le [et]	go [on a tour]
bsaddi2 [sadda2t]	believe
bsakkir [sakkart]	shut
bSammid [Sammadt]	save [money]
bSarrif [Sarraft]	exchange [money]
bSarrif [Sarraft lfi3l]	conjugate [verb]
bSawwir [Sawwart]	photo [take a]
bsee3id [see3adt]	help
bseefir [seefart]	travel
bsha33il [sha33alt]	turn on [oven]
bshuuf [shift]	see
bshuufak	see you later
bSi77 [Sa77ayt]	recover [health]
bsiir [sirt] / bSiir [Sirt]	become/happen
bsuu2 [si2t]	drive
btalfin [talfant]	phone [someone]
bTalli3 [Talla3t]	take up [luggage]
bTiir [Tirt]	fly
btitluj [talajit]	snow [vb]
buu2a3 [w2i3t]	fall
bukra	tomorrow
buuSal [wSilt]	arrive
bwarrid [warradt]	bloom/blossom
byi3jibne [3ajabne]	I like it
byi7ruz [7araz]	be worth it
byijiine [2ijeene]	receive
byiTla3 [Tili3] bi	amount to [bill]
bZammir [Zammart]	beep [toot]
bzarrik [zarrakt]	tease
bzuur [zirt]	visit
D3iif [D3aaf]	thin
Damiir [Damaayir]	pronoun
Damme	u [short vowel, as in foot]
Daruure [iyye]	necessary
Daww [2iDiwye]	light
Day3a [Diya3]	village
dayne [dineen]	ear
Di7k	laughter
diffeeye [et]	heater

GLOSSARY: LEBANESE - ENGLISH

Lebanese	English
dighre	straight ahead
dikkeen dkekiin	shop small
diin 2adyeen	religion
diine	religious/my religion
diwwayra et	circle
djeeje et\djeej	chicken
dolar aat	dollar
draama	drama
duush eet	shower
fa2iir a\fu2ara	poor
fann fnuun	art
fann mi3maare	architecture
farD fruuD	homework
farmashiyye et/Saydaliyye et	chemist
farruuj freriij	chicken grilled takeaway
farsh	furniture
faSl fSuul	season
faTbool	football
feekha fweeke	fruit
fetuura fwetiir	bill
fi	there is/are
fii ne\na\k\ke ...	be able to/can
fi3l 2af3aal	verb
fikra 2afkaar	idea
film 2afleem	film
film bi7azzin	tragedy
film biDa77ik	comedy
film buliise	detective film
film ri3b	horror
film romanse	romance
film tishwii2	thriller/suspense
film wasee2iQe	documentary
finjeen fnejiin	cup
finneen iin	artist
firsheeyit eet sneen	toothbrush
fisTaan fsaTiin	dress
foo2	on/above/over
fransa	France
fraaTa	coins/change
frinseewe iyye	French
garaaj eet	garage
garsoon eet	waiter
ghada	lunch
ghane 2aghniya	rich
gheer	another
ghirfe ghiraf	room
ghirfit noom	bedroom
ghisseele et	washing machine
ha abbr. for hayda\e\ool	this/these
halla2	now
hawa	air/ wind
haay	here is
hayda e\ool	this/these
hayi2tak	you seem to be
haykal hayeekil	temple
heek	that way
heek heek	so so
heek shi	something like that
heet ta	let's
hinne	they (are)
hiweeye et	hobby
hiyye	she (is)
hollanda	Holland
hollande iyye	Dutch
hoon	here
huniik	there/over there
huwwe	he (is)
jabal jbeel	mountain
jadwal jadeewil	table grid
jakeet teet	jacket
jariime jaraayim	crime
jaweeb 2ajwibe	answer
jaww	atmosphere
jdiid jdeed	new
jeelis	straight ahead
jeem3a at	university
jeemi3 jaweemi3	mosque
jibne 2ajbeen	cheese
jidd jduud	grandfather
jiheez 2ajhize kahrabee2e iyye	electrical appliance
jimle jimal	sentence
jnayne et	garden/park
jnayne wara lbeet	backyard
kafta	spiced meat usually served on a skewer
kalb kleeb	dog
kalimeet mit2aaT3a	crossword
kalse et	sock
kam +sg nn?	how many?/a few
kameen	also
kanabeeye et	sofa
kanze et	sweater
kariim kurama	generous
katidraa2iyye et	cathedral
kbiir kbaar	big
kenuun l2awwal	December
kenuun tteene	January
kees kyuus	glass for alcohol
keesak!	cheers! toast
kfeeye	enough
khabar 2akhbaar	news
khaadim khiddeem	servant
khalliilak lbee2e	keep the change
khalliina	let's
khamse	five
khaatim khaweetim	ring eg on finger
khaTT ghaami2	bold type
khaayif iin	afraid
khayy/2akh 2ikhwe	brother
kheeT khiTaan	string
khibz	bread
khidme et	service
khiDra	vegetables
khiTbe/khTuube	engagement
khood nafas	breathe/take it easy
khoof	fear nn
khzeene khazeeyin	cupboard
kibbe nayye	raw meat
kibbeeye et	glass general (no alcohol)

GLOSSARY: LEBANESE - ENGLISH

Lebanese	English
kiif?	how?
kiifak?	how are you?
kilfe [kilaf]	cost [nn]
kill [killkun]	all [all of you]
kill nnhaar	all day
killma	whenever/every time
kilme [kalimeet]	word
kirse [karaase]	chair
kniise [kaneeyis]	church
kteeb [kutub]	book
ktiir [adv]	very/a lot/much
ktiir [ktaar]	many [adj]
l2a7ad	Sunday
l2irb3a	Wednesday
l7amdilla	praise be to God
la [+vb/nn]	to/in order to/until
la ween?	where to?
la2	no
la2iim [lu2ama]	nasty [person]
la7m ba2ar	beef
la7m khanziir	pork
la7m kharuuf	lamb
la7me	meat
laff [eet]	turning [nn direction]
lakeen	in that case/then
lamma	when [in a statement]
laTiif [luTafa]	nice [person]
law	if
law ma	even if not
law7a [at]	painting
lawa7de [na\ak...]	alone
layle [layeele]	night
leel	night time
leesh?	why?
leezim	must/have to [+ verb]
li2ann [e\a\ak\ik...]	because [I\we\you]
li2anno	because
li3b lwara2	playing cards
libneen	Lebanon
libneene [iyye]	Lebanese
lighgha [at]	language
liistit [eet] lmashruub	menu [drink]
liistit l2akl	menu [food]
ljeey	next [month]
ljim3a	Friday
lkhamiis	Thursday
lkhariif	autumn
lkheerij	abroad
lkill	everyone
lmarra ljeey	next time
loon [2alween]	colour
lyabaan	Japan
lyoom	today
m3allabeet	canned foods
m3allim [iin]	teacher/sir/waiter
m7aTTa [at]	station
m7aTTit ttreen	train station
ma	don't [didn't/won't: negates verb]
ma 3ada	except
ma heek?	right?/isn't that so?
ma yhimmak	don't worry
ma2kuleet ba7riyye	seafood
ma3	with
ma3 i ssaleeme	bye [person staying]
ma3juun sneen	toothpaste
ma3lam [ma3aalim]	landmark
ma3leesh/ma bihimm	never mind
ma3raD fanne	art gallery
ma3raD [ma3aariD]	exhibition
ma7all [eet]	shop/room
mabna [mabeene]	building
mabna turaase [iyye]	heritage building
mabSuuT [iin]	happy
maaDe [yiin]	past/last
madrase [madeeris]	school
mahbuul [mhebiil]	dumb
makhbuuz [iin]	baked
makhfar shshirTa	police station
maktab l2isti3lemeet	reception desk
maktab [makeetib]	office
maktabe [et]	bookshop
mal3uun [mle3iin]	crafty
malyoon [mleyiin]	million
man2uushe [mne2iish]	herb pizza
manishfe [maneeshif]	towel
manTa2a [manaaTi2]	area
manZar [manaaZir]	view
mar7aba	hello
mara [nisween]	woman
mariiD [muraDa]	sick
markab [mareekib]	boat
marra	time/once
masa	evening
masa lkheer	good evening
masalan	for example
maSaare	money
masba7 [maseebi7]	swimming pool
mashe	on foot
mashghuul [iin]	busy
mashruub [eet]	drink
masluu2	boiled
masruu2	stolen
maT3am [maTaa3im]	restaurant
mat7af fanne	art gallery
mat7af [matee7if]	museum
maTaar [aat]	airport
maTbakh [maTaabikh]	kitchen
maTbuukh	cooked
maw2i3 [mawee2i3]	site
maw2if lbaaS	stop [bus/train...]
maw3id [mawa3iid]	meeting/appointment
mawze [mooz]	banana
maaycroweeyv [eet]	microwave
mbeeri7	yesterday
mdiine [mudun]	city
meeshe l7aal	things are fine
meeza	meze [entree of many little dishes]
mghanne [iyye]	singer

GLOSSARY: LEBANESE - ENGLISH

mghayyim	cloudy
mhandis iin	engineer
mi2le	fried
midde	while a
milyaar aat	billion
min	from/of/ago
min faDlak	please if you
min ween?	where from?
mish	not negates adjective/noun
misheen	for sone / so that
mishikle masheekil	problem
mishmis	sunny
mishwe iyye	grilled
mista2bal	future
mistashfa yeet	hospital
mit2akhkhir iin	late
mit2akkid iin	sure/certain
mitl l3aade	as usual
mitwassiT iin	medium
miyye et	hundred
mmarriD iin	nurse
mneesib iin	appropriate
mnii7 mnee7	good/fine/well
mobaayl eet	mobile phone
mool	shopping centre
motorsiikl	motorbike
mrabba	jam
mreeye et	mirror
mshaghghil CD/DVD	player CD/DVD
mtabbal iin	marinated
mu2abbileet/meeza	entree/appetisers
mu7aame iyye	lawyer
mu7iiT aat	ocean
mughaamara at	adventure
muhim iin	important
mukhaaTara makhaaTir	risk
mumill iin	boring
murii7 iin	comfortable
musii2a	music
mwaZZaf iin l2oteel	hotel attendant
na2l	moving house
na3am	yes polite
nafs/zeet	same
nashaaT aat	activity
naaSi7 iin	fat
nayy	raw
naZar	vision
nbiid	wine
nDiif nDaaf	clean
nees	people
nhaar nharaat	day/daytime
nhaarak sa3iid	good day
ni7na	we (are)
niheeyit l2usbuu3	weekend
nimra nimar	number
niseen	April
nishkur 2alla	God be thanked
nishsheefe et	dryer
niSS nSuuS	half

niyyeelak!	lucky you!
njaaSa njaaS	pear
noo3 2anwee3	genre/type
nshalla	God willing
numuuzaj nameezij	model
ra2m 2ar2aam	number
ra2y 2araa2	opinion
ra7	will/going to + vb
rasm eet	drawing/painting
raayi7 2ishitre kam gharaD	go shopping
raayi7 a\7iin 3a	going to
rfii2 rif2a	friend/companion
rib3 2arbee3	quarter
riDa	satisfaction
rijjeel rjeel	man/waiter
riweeye et	novel
rizz	rice
rmeede iyye	grey
rrabii3	spring
rumeene iyye	roman
ruuse ruus	Russian
rusiyya	Russia
ryaaDa	sports
Sa3b	difficult
Sa77teen	bon appetit enjoy your meal
Sa7n S7uun	plate/dish
sab3a	seven
Sabaa7 lkheer	good morning
Sabe Sibyeen	boy
Sabuune Sabuun	soap
Sadii2 2aSdiQaa2	friend
safar	travel
Saff Sfuuf	class(room)
Saakhin iin	sick
saleemtak	wish I/we you a speedy recovery
sallim sallmo	give my/our regards
Saloon eet	living/lounge room
samke samak	fish
saandwish eet	sandwich
sarii3 iin	fast
sawa	together
SayDaliyye et	chemist
see3a at	hour/o'clock
see7a at	square of city/village
Seed	hunting
Seed ssamak	fishing
seekin iin	live
seeyi7 siwwee7	tourist
shahr 2ashhor	month
shajra shajar	tree
shakhS 2ashkhaaS	person
shams shmuus	sun
shanta shinat	bag
shaaTir iin	clever
shaay	tea
shbaaT	February
sheeri3 shaweeri3	street
shi 2ishya	thing/something

GLOSSARY: LEBANESE - ENGLISH

Lebanese	English
shi 3ajiib!	amazing!
shi marra	ever
shi yoom	one day
shi22a [shi2a2]	apartment
shibbeek [shbebiik]	window
shighil [2ashghaal]	work
shirke [shirak]	company
shiish [shyeesh]	skewer
shite	rain [nn]
shite khafiif	drizzle
shmeel	left
shoob	hot
shoorba	soup
shoort [eet]	shorts
shsheem/dimash2	Damascus
shshite	winter
shu 2awlak?	what do you think?
shu beek [kun]?	what's wrong?
shu ra2yak?	what do you think?
shu?	what?
shukran	thank you
shwayy	a little
Sib7	morning
SibbaaT [SbabiiT]	shoes
sikkar	sugar
sinama [eet]	cinema
Siine [Siin]	Chinese
sine [sniin]	year
sitt [eet]	lady/waitress
sitt [eet]	grandmother
sitte	six
siyyaara [at]	car
skotlanda	Scotland
skotlande [iyye]	Scottish
slaaTa [at]	salad
Soob	towards
spanyoole [spanyool]	Spanish
ssabt	Saturday
SSeef	summer
SSiin	China
stuudyo [weet]	studio
suu2 [2aswee2]	market
su2aal [2as2ila]	question
suppermaarket	supermarket
Suura [Suwar]	photo/picture
T7iin	flour
ta [+vb]	to/in order to/until
ta2m [t2uume]	suit [mn]
Ta2s	weather
ta7t	under/below
Tab3an	of course
Tabii3a	nature
takht [tkhuute]	bed
taksi	taxi
talfizyoon [eet]	television
Taalib [Tillaab]	student
talifoon [eet]	phone
talj	snow
tammuuz	July
tanke [tanak]	can
tasawwo2	shopping
Tawiil [Twaal]	tall/long
Tayyib	ok
Tayyib [iin]	tasty
teene [ye\yiin]	another
tenis	tennis
teriikh [taweriikh]	date/history
teriikhe [iyye]	historical
tfaDDal [e\o]	Please / here you are (inviting sone to do sthg eg eat/enter...)
ti3been [e\iin]	tired
Tibbaakh [iin]	cook
tiffee7a [tiffee7]	apple
tikram [e\o/7aaDir inv.]	sure before fulfilling sone's wish
tilt	third
tilyeene [tilyeen]	Italian
timriin [tameriin]	exercise
timseel [tamesiil]	statue
tirwii2a	breakfast
tis3a	nine
tishriin l2awwal	October
tishriin tteene	November
tisjiil [eet]	recording
Tiyyaara [at]	plane
tleete	three
tmeene	eight
tnayneetna [kun]	both of us [you p]
tneen/tinteen [o'clock]	two
treen [eet]	train
tsharrafna/2ahlan	pleased to meet you
ttaleeta	Tuesday
ttaneen	Monday
turaase	heritage
tuut	berry
tyeeb/maleebis	clothes
w	and
wa2t [2aw2aat]	time/period of time
wa2t lfaraagh	spare time
waa7ad [wi7de]	one
wa7iid [e]	only child
wajbe khafiife	snack
wajbe ra2iisiyye	main meal
wajbe [et]	meal
walad [wleed]	child
walla	or
waLLa	by God
war2a [wraa2]	paper/leaf
wara	behind
waSat limdiine	city centre
wasee2il nna2l	means of transport
waSf/na3t	adjective
waTane	national/my nation
weelid [e/2ahl]	parent
ween?	where?
weenma [+ verb]	wherever
weenma keen	everywhere/wherever
wisikh [iin]	dirty
ya	oh [+name esp. to attract sone's attention]

GLOSSARY: LEBANESE - ENGLISH

ya ... ya ...	either ... or ...
ya3ne	means
yabaane [yabaan]	Japanese
yakhne	stew
yaLLa	let's go
yalle [in a statement]	that/which/who
yamiin	right[direction]
yasaar	left[direction]
yimkin	maybe
yoom [2iyyeem]	day/24 hours
yoom l2a7ad	Sunday[on]
yoom ssabt	Saturday[on]
Zahra [zhuur]	flower
zake [2azkiya]	intelligent
Zarf	adverb
zeet [zyuut]	oil
zeet/nafs	same
zeeyir [zuwwaar]	visitor
zghiir [zghaar]	small
zibde	butter
zikra	anniversary
zoo2/zaw2 [ak...]	taste

GLOSSARY: ENGLISH - LEBANESE

GLOSSARY

ENGLISH	LEBANESE
able to/can	fii$^{ne\backslash na\backslash k\backslash ke...}$
abroad	lkheerij
across the road from	2iddeem
action	7adas^{2a7dees}
activity	nashaaT^{aat}
address	3inween^{3anawiin}
adjective	waSf/na3t
adore[I] that sort of thing	bmuut bi heek shi
adventure	mughaamara^{at}
adverb	Zarf
afraid	khaayif^{iin}
after	ba3idma^{+vb}
after	ba3d
afternoon [in the]	ba3d i DDohr
afterwards	ba3deen
ago	min
air	hawa
airport	maTaar^{aat}
all day	kill nnhaar
all [of you]	kill^{kun}
alone	lawa7de$^{na\backslash ak...}$
also	kameen
amazing!	shi 3ajiib!
America	2ameerka
American	2amerkeene
amount to [bill]	byiTla3^{Tili3} bi
ancient ruins	2asaraat 2adiime
and	w
anniversary	zikra
another	teene$^{\backslash ye\backslash yiin}$
answer	jaweeb^{2ajwibe}
anymore	ba2a
apartment	shi22a^{shi2a2}
appetisers	mu2abbileet/meeza
apple	tiffee7a^{tiffee7}
appointment [make an]	beekhud maw3id
appropriate/suitable	mneesib^{iin}
April	niseen
Arabic	3arabe
arak	3ara2
architecture	fann mi3maare
area	manTa2a^{manaaTi2}
around	7awla/7aweele
arrive	buuSal^{wSilt}
art	fann^{fnuun}
art gallery	ma3raD fanne
artist	finneen^{iin}
as usual	mitl l3aade
ask	bis2al^{sa2alt}
at all	2abadan
at Layla's	3ind layla
at your leisure/as you please	3ala raa7tak
atmosphere	jaww^{2ajwee2}
attention	2intibeeh
August	2aab
Australia	2ostraalya
Australian	2ostraale^{iyye}
autumn	lkhariif
backyard	jnayne wara lbeet
bad	3aaTil^{iin}
bag	shanta^{shinat}
baked	makhbuuz^{iin}
baklava	ba2leewa
balcony	balkoon^{blekiin}
banana	mawze^{mooz}
bath(tub)	baanyo
bathroom	7immeem^{eet}
be [was]	bkuun^{kint}
be worth it	byi7ruz^{7araz}
beautiful	7ilo$^{7ilwe\backslash iin}$
because	li2anno
because [I\we\you]	li2anne$^{na\backslash ak\backslash ik...}$
become	bsiir^{sirt} / bSir^{Sirt}
become tearful	bitdammi3^{damma3it} 3ayne
bed	takht^{tkhuute}
bedroom	ghirfit noom
beef	la7m ba2ar
beep [toot]	bZammir^{Zammart}
beer	biira
before	2abilma^{+vb}
before/in advance	2abl
beginning	bideeyee^{t}
behind	wara
believe	bsaddi2^{sadda2t}
berry	tuut
better	2afDal
between	been
bicycle	bisikleet^{eet}
big	kbiir^{kbaar}
bill	fetuura^{fwetiir}
billion	milyaar^{aat}
birthday	3iid mileed
black	2aswad$^{sawda\backslash suud}$
bloom/blossom	bwarrid^{warradt}
blue	2azra2$^{zar2a\backslash zir2}$
boat	markab^{mareekib}
boiled	masluu2
bold type	khaTT ghaami2
bon appétit [enjoy your meal]	Sa77teen
book	kteeb^{kutub}
book [trip]	bi7juz^{7ajazt}
bookshop	maktabe^{et}
boring	mumill^{iin}
both of [us/you p]	tnayneet$^{na/kun}$
bottle	2anniine^{2aneene}
boy	Sabe^{Sibyeen}
brackets [in]	been 2oSeen
bread	khibz
break	biksur^{kasart}
breakfast	tirwii2a
breathe/take it easy	khood nafas
bring	bjiib^{jibt}
brother	2akh/khayy^{2ikhwe}
brown	binne^{binniyye}

GLOSSARY: ENGLISH - LEBANESE

English	Lebanese
building	mabna[mabeene]
bus	2otobiis[eet]/ baaS[eet]/ booSTa[at]
busy	mashghuul[iin]
but	bas
butter	zibde
buy	bishitre[shtarayt/shtriit]
by God	waLLa
bye [person leaving]	bkhaaTrak
bye [person staying]	ma3 i ssaleeme
cafe	2ahwe[2aheewe]
cake	7ilo[7ilweyeet]
call out to	b3ayyiT[3ayyaTt] la
can	tanke[tanak]
can/able to	bi2dir[2dirt]
canned foods	m3allabeet
capital	3aaSme[3awaaSim]
car	siyyaara[at]
cathedral	katidraa2iyye[et]
CD player	mshaghghil CD
chair	kirse[karaase]
change [money]	lbee2e
cheers! [toast]	keesak!
cheese	jibne[2ajbeen]
chemist	farmashiyyee[t]/SayDaliyyee[t]
chicken	djeejee[t\djeej]
chicken [grilled takeaway]	farruuj[freriij]
chickpeas	7ummuS
child	walad[wleed]
China	SSiin
Chinese	Siine[Siin]
choose	bna22e[na22ayt]/bikhtaar[khtart]
church	kniise[kaneeyis]
cinema	sinama[eet]
circle	diwwayra[at]
city	mdiine[mudun]
city centre	waSat limdiine
class(room)	Saff [Sfuuf]
clean	nDiif[nDaaf]
clever	shaaTir[iin]
close/near (to)	2ariib[2raab] (min)
clothes	tyeeb/maleebis
cloudy	mghayyim
coffee	2ahwe[2aheewe]
coins	fraaTa
cold	bard
colour	loon[2alween]
come	bije[jiit]
comedy	film biDa77ik
comfortable	murii7[iin]
companion/friend	rfii2[rif2a]
company	shirke[shirak]
complete [vb]	bkammil[kammalt]
concern	2ihtimeem
conjugate [verb]	bSarrif[Sarraft] lfi3l
conjunction [and/but/or...]	7arf 3aTf
consonant	7arf seekin
contact	bittiSil[ttaSalt]
converse	bit7addas[t7addast]

English	Lebanese
cook	biTbukh[Tabakht]
cook	Tibbaakh[iin]
cooked	maTbuukh
cost [(its) vb]	bikallif[kallaf]
cost [nn]	kilfe[kilaf]
country	balad[bleed/bildeen]
crafty	mal3uun[mle3iin]
crime	jariime[jaraayim]
criticise	binti2id[nta2adt]
cross [street]	bi2Ta3[2aTa3t]
crossword	kalimeet mit2aaT3a
cup	finjeen[fnejiin]
cupboard	khzeene[khazeeyin]
currency	3imle[et]
Damascus	shsheem/dimash2
darkness	3atm
date/history	teriikh[taweriikh]
day after tomorrow	ba3d bukra
day before yesterday	2awwilt mbeeri7
day/24 hours	yoom[2iyyeem]
day/daytime	nhaar[nharaat]
dear [my] /love[my]	7abiibee[te]
December	kenuun l2awwal
dessert	7ilo[7ilweyeet]
detective	film buliise
dictate/give orders	bi7kum[7akamt]
difficult	Sa3b
dinner	3asha
dirty	wisikh[iin]
discover	biktishif[ktashaft]
dish	Sa7n[S7uun]
distract	bilhe[lahayt/lhiit]
do	ba3mul[3milt]
doctor	7akiim[7ukama]
documentary	film wasee2iQe
dog	kalb[kleeb]
dollar	dolar[aat]
don't muck around/mock	bala maSkhara
don't worry	ma yhimmak
door	beeb[bweeb]
drama	draama
draw [picture]	birsum[rasamt]
drawing	rasm[eet]
dress	fisTaan[fsaTiin]
drink [nn]	mashruub[eet]
drink [vb]	bishrab[shribt]
drive	bsuu2[si2t]
drizzle [nn]	shite khafiif
drizzle [vb]	bitshatte 3a lkhafiif
dryer	nishsheefe[et]
dumb	mahbuul[mhebiil]
Dutch	hollande [iyye]
ear	dayne[dineen]
early	bakkiir
eat	beekul[2akalt]
eggplant	batinjeen
eight	tmeene
either ... or ...	ya ... ya ...

GLOSSARY: ENGLISH - LEBANESE

English	Lebanese
electrical appliance	jiheez[2ajhize] kahrabee2e[iyye]
electronics	2elektroniyyeet
engagement	khiTbe/khTuube
engineer	mhandis[iin]
England	2ingliteerra
English	2ingliize[2ingliiz]
enjoy [have a good time]	binbiSit[nbaSatt]
enough	bikaffe[kaffa]
enough	kfeeye
enter	bfuut[fitt]
entree	mu2abbileet
Europe	2orooppa
even	7atta
even if not	law ma
evening	masa
event	7adas[2a7dees]
ever	shi marra
everyone	lkill
everywhere/wherever	weenma keen
exactly	biZZabt
except	ma 3ada
exchange [money]	bSarrif[Sarraft]
excuse me	3afwan[inv.]
exercise	timriin[tameriin]
exhibit [an]	3arD[3ruuD]
exhibition	ma3raD[ma3aariD]
exhibits [objects]	2ishya ma3ruuDa
expression/phrase	3ibaara[at]
faint [lose consciousness]	bighiTT[ghaTT] 3a 2albe
fall	buu2a3[w2i3t]
fall asleep	bighfa[ghfiit]
family	3ayle[3iyal]
far [from]	b3iid[b3aad] (3an)
fast	sarii3[iin]
fat	naaSi7[iin]
father	2ab[aweet]/ bayy[eet]
fear [nn]	khoof
February	shbaaT
fill in	b3ambe[3ambayt]
film	film[2afleem]
finally	2akhiiran
fine [things are / I'm...]	meeshe l7aal
fine/good	mnii7[mnee7]
finish	bikhlaS[khalaSt/khliSt]
first thing/of all	2awwal shi
fish	samke[samak]
fishing	Seed ssamak
five	khamse
flask	baT7a[at]
flour	T7iin
flower	zahra[zhuur]
fly	bTiir[Tirt]
follow	bitba3[taba3t]
food	2akl[ma2kuleet]
football	faTbool
for example	masalan
for someone/so that	misheen
forget	binsa[nsiit]

English	Lebanese
four	2arb3a
France	fransa
French	frinseewe[iyye]
Friday	ljim3a
fridge	birraad[eet]
fried	mi2le
friend	Sadii2[2aSdiQaa2]
from	min
fruit	feekha[fweeke]
full [be, of food]	bishba3[shbi3t]
furniture	farsh
future	mista2bal
garage	garaaj[eet]
garden	jnayne[et]/7adii2a[7adeeyi2]
general	3aamm
generous	kariim[kurama]
German	2almaane
Germany	2almaanya
get drunk	biskar[skirt]
get married	bitjawwaz[tjawwazt]
get off [bus]	binzal[nzilt]
get up [out of bed]	b2uum[2imt]
get wet	binball[nballayt]
girl	bint[baneet]
give	ba3Te[3aTayt/3Tiit]
give my/our regards	sallim[sallme\o]
glass [for alcohol]	kees[kyuus]
glass [general]	kibbeeye[et]
go for a walk	bitmashsha[tmashshayt]
go [on a tour]	bruu7[ri7t] ra7le[et]
go out	biDhar[Dahart/Dhirt]
go shopping	raayi7 2ishitre kam gharaD
go to	bruu7[ri7t] 3a
God be thanked	nishkur 2alla
God willing	nshalla
going to	raayi7[a\7iin] 3a
going to/will + vb	ra7
good day	nhaarak sa3iid
good evening	masa lkheer
good morning	Sabaa7 lkheer
good/fine/well	mnii7[a\mnee7]
grandfather	jidd[jduud]
grandmother	sitt[eet]
green	2akhDar[khaDra\khiDr]
grey	rmeede[iyye]
grilled	mishwe[iyye]
hairdresser	7illaa2[iin]
half	niSS[nSuuS]
happen	bSiir[Sirt]/bsiir[sirt]
happy	mabSuuT[iin]
hat	birnayTa[braniiT]
have breakfast	bitrawwa2[trawwa2t]
have to [+ verb]	leezim
have [you]	3indak
he (is)	huwwe
hear	bisma3[smi3t]
heater	diffeeye[et]
hello	mar7aba

GLOSSARY: ENGLISH - LEBANESE

English	Lebanese
hello	2ahlan
help	bsee3id [see3adt]
herb pizza	man2uushe [mne2iish]
here	hoon
here is	haay
heritage	turaase
heritage building	mabna turaase [iyye]
hide	bkhabbe [khabbayt]
historical	teriikhe [iyye]
hobby	hiweeye [et]
holiday	3iTlee [t]
Holland	hollanda
homework	farD [fruuD]
horror film	film ri3b
hospital	mistashfa [yeet]
hot [weather]	shoob
hotel attendant	mwaZZaf [iin] l2oteel
hour/o'clock	see3a [at]
house	beet [byuut]
how are you?	kiifak?
how many?	kam [+sg nn]?
how much [cost]?	b2addesh?
how much [time/distance]?	2addeesh [ssee3a/lmaseefe]?
how?	kiif?
hundred	miyye [et]
hunting	Seed
I (am)	2ana
I like it	byi3jibne [3ajabne]
idea	fikra [2afkaar]
if [can happen]	2iza
if [not happening/didn't happen]	law
important	muhimm [iin]
in	bi
in front of	2iddeem
in that case/then	lakeen
in three years	ba3d [tleet sniin]
ing [suffix]	3am [prefix equivalent to verb+ing suffix in English]
injure/wound	bijra7 [jara7t]
intelligent	zake [2azkiya]
interesting	7ilo [7ilwe\iin]
internet	2internet
invitation	3aziime [3azeeyim]
invite	bi3zum [3azamt]
Ireland	2irlanda
Irish	2irlande [iyye]
Italian	tilyeene [tilyeen]
Italy	2iTaalya
jacket	jakeet [teet]
jam	mrabba
January	kenuun tteene
Japan	lyabaan
Japanese	yabaane [yabaan]
juice	3aSiir [3aSaayir]
July	tammuuz
June	7zayraan
just	bas
keep the change	khalliilak lbee2e
kitchen	maTbakh [maTaabikh]
know	ba3rif [3rift]
lamb	la7m kharuuf
landmark	ma3lam [ma3aalim]
language	lighgha [at]
last	2eekhir [iin]
late	mit2akhkhir [iin]
laughter	Di7k
lawyer	mu7aame [iyye]
learn	bit3allam [t3allamt]
leave	bitruk [tarakt]
Lebanese	libneene [iyye]
Lebanon	libneen
left [direction]	yasaar/shmeel
let's	heet ta / khalliina
let's go	yaLLa
letter [of alphabet]	7arf [7ruuf]
lie [be dishonest]	bikzub [kazabt]
light	Daww [2iDiwye]
like	b7ibb [7abbayt]
listen	bitsamma3 [tsamma3t]
little [adj]	2aliil [2leel]
little [adv]	shwayy
live	seekin [e\iin]
living/lounge room	Saloon [eet]
long	Tawiil [Twaal]
look	bitTalla3 [TTalla3t]
loosen	brakhkhe [rakhkhayt]
love	b7ibb [7abbayt]
lucky you!	niyyeelak!
lunch	ghada
main meal	wajbe ra2iisiyye
man	rijjeel [rjeel]
many [adj]	ktiir [ktaar]
March	2adaar
marinated	mtabbal [iin]
market	suu2 [2aswee2]
May	2ayyaar
maybe	barke/balke
maybe	yimkin
meal	wajbe [t]
means [it]	ya3ne
means of transport	wasee2il nna2l
meat	la7me
medium	mitwassiT [iin]
meet up	bitlee2a [tlee2ayt]
meeting/appointment	maw3id [mawa3iid]
menu [drink]	liistit [eet] lmashruub
menu [food]	liistit l2akl
meze [entree of many little dishes]	meeza
microwave	maaycroweeyv [eet]
million	malyoon [mleyiin]
mirror	mreeye [et]
mobile phone	mobaayl [eet]
model	numuuzaj [nameezij]
Monday	ttaneen
money	maSaare
month	shahr [2ashhor]
moon	2amar [2maar]

GLOSSARY: ENGLISH - LEBANESE

English	Lebanese
morning	Sib7
mosque	jeemi3^(jaweemi3)
mother	2imm^(eet)
motorbike	motorsiikl^(eet)
mountain	jabal^(jbeel)
move house	bin2ul^(na2alt)
moving house	na2l^(nn)
much	ktiir^(adv)
museum	mat7af^(matee7if)
music	musii2a
must	leezim
name	2ism^(2aseeme)
nasty ^(person)	la2iim^(lu2ama)
national/my nation	waTane
nature	Tabii3a
near	2ariib^(e\2raab)
necessary	Daruure^(iyye)
never mind	ma3leesh/ma bihimm
new	jdiid^(jdeed)
news	khabar^(2akhbaar)
next ^(eg month)	ljeey
next time	lmarra ljeey
next to	7add
nice ^(person)	laTiif^(luTafa)
nice ^(thing)	7ilo^(7ilwe\iin)
night	layle^(layeele)
night time	leel
nine	tis3a
no	la2
not	ma^(negates verb)
not	mish^(negates adjective/noun)
novel	riweeye^(et)
November	tishriin tteene
now	halla2
number	nimra^(nimar)/ra2m^(2ar2aam)
nurse	mmarriD^(iin)
ocean	mu7iiT^(aat)
October	tishriin l2awwal
of	min
of course	Tab3an
office	maktab^(makeetib)
oh	ya^(+name esp to attract sn's attention)
oil	zeet^(zyuut)
ok	Tayyib
old	3atii2^(3tee2) / 2adiim^(2deem)
on	3a/3ala
on foot	mashe
on the contrary	bi l3aks
on ^(the third of August)	bi^(tleete 2aab)
on/above/over	foo2
one	waa7ad^(wi7de)
one day	shi yoom
only child	wa7iid^(e)
open	bifta7^(fata7t)
opinion	ra2y^(2araa2)
or	2aw/walla
orange	bird2aane^(bird2aan)
order ^(drink/food)	biTlub^(Talabt)
origin ^(country of)	2aSl
other	gheer
outside	barra
paint ^(eg house)	biTrush^(Tarasht)
painting	law7a^(at)
pants	banTaloon^(bnaTliin)
paper/leaf	war2a^(wraa2)
parent	weelid^(e\2ahl)
park/garden	7adii2a^(7adeeyi2)/jnayne^(et)
past	maaDe
past/last	maaDe^(yiin)
pay	bidfa3^(dafa3t)
pay attention	bintibih^(ntabaht)
pear	njaaSa^(njaaS)
pen	2alam^(2leem)
pencil	2alam rSaaS
people	nees
person	shakhS^(2ashkhaaS)
perspire	bi3ra2^(3ri2t)
phone ^(nn)	talifoon^(eet)
phone ^(vb)	btalfin^(talfant)
photo	Suura^(Suwar)
photo ^(vb)	bSawwir^(Sawwart)
picture	Suura^(Suwar)
piece	2iT3a^(2iTa3)
piece of cake	2iT3it 7ilo
plan	bkhaTTit^(khaTTat)
plane	Tiyyaara^(at)
plate	Sa7n^(S7uun)
play	bil3ab^(l3ibt)
playing cards	li3b lwara2
please ^(if you)	min faDlak / law sama7t / 2iza bitriid / 3mool ma3ruuf
Please / here you are ^((inviting sone to eat/enter...))	tfaDDal^(e\o)
pleased to meet you	tsharrafna/2ahlan
police station	makhfar shshirTa
polish ^(shoes)	blammi3^(lamma3t)
poor	fa2iir^(a\fu2ara)
poor thing!	7araam!
pork	la7m khanziir
praise be to God	l7amdilla
prefer	bfaDDil^(faDDalt)
preposition ^(in/on/at...)	7arf jarr
present	7aaDir^(iin)
problem	mishkle^(masheekil)
pronoun	Damiir^(Damaayir)
quarter	rib3^(2arbee3)
question	su2aal^(2as2ila)
quickly	bi sir3a
rain ^(nn)	shite
rain ^(vb)	bitshatte^(shattit)
raw	nayy
raw meat	kibbe nayye
read	bi2ra^(2riit)
ready	7aaDir^(iin)
receive	byijiine^(2ijeene)
reception desk	maktab l2isti3lemeet

GLOSSARY: ENGLISH - LEBANESE

English	Lebanese
recording	tisjiil^{eet}
recover ^{health}	bishfa^{shfiit}/ bSi77^{Sa77ayt}
red	2a7mar$^{7amra\7umr}$
regret	bindam^{ndimt}
relative $^{extended\ family}$	2ariib^{2raayib}
relax/rest	birtee7^{rta7t}
religion	diin^{2adyeen}
religious	diine
remainder/rest	lbee2e
repeat	b3iid^{3idt}
restaurant	maT3am^{maTaa3im}
return	birja3^{rji3t}
rice	rizz
rich	ghane^{2aghniya}
right ^{direction}	yamiin
right/isn't that so?	ma heek?
ring	khaatim^{khaweetim}
risk	mukhaaTara^{makhaaTir}
robbed ^{get}	binsiri2^{nsara2t}
roman	rumeene^{iyye}
romance $^{film/novel}$	romanse
room	ghirfe^{ghiraf}
room ^{space}	ma7all^{eet}
rope	7abl^{7beel}
ruins	2asaraat
Russia	rusiyya
Russian	ruuse^{ruus}
sad	7aziin^{iin}
sadness	7izn^{2a7zeen}
salad	slaaTa^{at}
same	zeet/nafs
sandwich	saandwish^{eet}
satisfaction	riDa
Saturday	ssabt
Saturday ^{on}	yoom ssabt
save ^{money}	bSammid^{Sammadt}
say	b2uul^{2ilt}
scare	bkhawwif^{khawwaft}
school	madrase^{madeeris}
Scotland	skotlanda
Scottish	skotlande^{iyye}
sea	ba7r^{b7uur}
seafood	ma2kuleet ba7riyye
season	faSl^{fSuul}
see	bshuuf^{shift}
see ^{film}	bi7Dar^{7Dirt}
see you later	bshuufak
seem ^{you} to be	hayi2tak
send	bib3at^{ba3att}
sentence	jimle^{jimal}
September	2ayluul
servant	khaadim^{khiddeem}
serve/be of service	bikhdum^{khadamt}
service	khidme^{khadameet}
seven	sab3a
shame(ful)	3ayb
she (is)	hiyye
shirt	2amiiS^{2imSaan}
shoes	SibbaaT^{SbabiiT}
shop	dikkeen^{dkekiin}/ma7all^{eet}
shopping	tasawwo2
shopping centre	mool
short	2aSiir^{2Saar}
short story	2iSSa 2aSiire
shorts	shoort^{eet}
shower	duush^{eet}
shut	bsakkir^{sakkart}
sick	mariiD^{muraDa}/ Saakhin^{iin}
silent ^{be}	biskut^{sakatt}
singer	mghanne^{iyye}
singlet	broteel^{eet}
sister	2ikht^{2ikhweet}
sit down	bi23ud^{2a3adt}
site	maw2i3^{mawee2i3}
six	sitte
skate	bitzallaj^{tzallajt}
skewer	shiish^{shyeesh}
ski	bitzallaj^{tzallajt}
sleep	bneem^{nimt}
sleepy	bin3as^{n3ist}/ni3seen
slow	baTii2^{iin}
slowly ^{go}	3a mihlak
small	zghiir^{zghaar}
snack	wajbe khafiife
snow ^{nn}	talj
snow ^{vb}	btitluj^{talajit}
so so	heek heek
so that	7atta
soap	Sabuune^{Sabuun}
sock-s	kalse^{et}
sofa	kanabeeye^{et}
solution	7all^{7luul}
some	kam
something	shi^{2ishya}
something like that	heek shi
soon	2ariiban
sorry	bi3tizir^{3tazart}
soup	shoorba
Spain	2espaanya
Spanish	spanyoole^{spanyool}
spare time	wa2t lfaraagh
speak	bi7ke^{7kiit}
spend ^{money}	biSruf^{Saraft}
spend ^{time}	b2aDDE^{2aDDayt}
spiced meat $^{usually\ served\ on\ a\ skewer}$	kafta
sports	ryaaDa
spring	rrabii3
square $^{of\ city/village}$	see7a^{at}
stand	biw2af^{w2ift}
start	bballish^{ballasht}
station	m7aTTa^{at}
statue	timseel^{tamesiil}
stay $^{eg\ in\ hotel}$	binzal^{nzilt}
stay $^{in\ a\ city/hotel}$	bib2a^{b2iit}/ bi23ud^{2a3adt}
staying $^{eg\ in\ hotel}$	bee2e^{yiin}
steal	bisru2^{sara2t}

GLOSSARY: ENGLISH - LEBANESE

English	Lebanese
stew	yakhne
stingy	bakhiil[bukhala]
stolen	masruu2
stop [nn bus/train...]	maw2if[mawee2if] lbaaS
stop [vb]	biw2af[w2ift]
storm	3aaSfe[3awaaSif]
story	2iSSa[2iSSaS]
straight ahead	dighre/ jeelis
street	sheeri3[shaweeri3]
string	kheeT[khiTaan]
strong	2awe[2weeya]
stuck [be, in a place]	binzirib[nzarabt]
student	Taalib[Tillaab]
studio	stuudyo[weet]
sugar	sikkar
suit [eg clothes]	ta2m[t2uume]
suit [vb]	bineesib[neesab]
summer	SSeef
sun	shams[shmuus]
Sunday	l2a7ad
Sunday [on]	yoom l2a7ad
sunny	mishmis
supermarket	suppermaarket
sure [before fulfilling sone's wish]	tikram[e\o]/7aaDir[inv.]
sure/certain	mit2akkid[iin]
sweater	kanze[et]
swim	bisba7[saba7t]
swimming pool	masba7[maseebi7]
table [grid]	jadwal[jadeewil]
take	beekhud[2akhadt]
take up [luggage]	bTalli3[Talla3t]
tall	Tawiil[Twaal]
tan	bismarr[smarrayt]
taste	zoo2/zaw2[ak...]
tasty	Tayyib[iin]
taxi	taksi
tea	shaay
teacher/sir	m3allim[iin]/2isteez[2aseetze]
tease	bzarrik[zarrakt]
television	talfizyoon[eet]
tell	bi7ke[7kiit]
temple	haykal[hayeekil]
ten	3ashra
tennis	tenis
thank	bishkur[shakart]
thank you	shukran
that	2inno
that way	heek
that/which	yalle
there is/are	fi
there/over there	huniik
these	haydool / ha
they (are)	hinne
thin	D3iif[D3aaf]
things	shi[2ishya]
think	biftikir[ftakart]
third	tilt
this	hayda[e\ool]/ha
this/these	ha[abbr. for hayda\e\ool]
thousand	2alf[2lufeet]
three	tleete
thriller/suspense	film tishwii2
Thursday	lkhamiis
till	7atta
time/once	marra
time/period of time	wa2t[2aw2aat]
tired	ti3been[e\iin]
to [after verb eg I wanted to]	2inne[na/ak...]
to/in order to/until	ta[+vb] / la[+vb/nn]
to/minus [time]	2illa
toast [in celebration]	bishrab[shribt] kees
today	lyoom
together	sawa
toilet	7immeem[eet]
tomorrow	bukra
toothbrush	firsheeyit sneen
toothpaste	ma3juun sneen
tourist	seeyi7[siwwee7]
towards	Soob
towel	manishfe[maneeshif]
tragedy	film bi7azzin
train	treen[eet]
train station	m7aTTit ttreen
travel [nn]	safar
travel [vb]	bseefir[seefart]
tree	shajra[shajar]
try on	bjarrib[jarrabt]
Tuesday	ttaleeta
turn on [oven]	bsha33il[sha33alt]
turn [vb]	bliff[laffayt]
turning [nn direction]	laff[eet]
two	tneen/tinteen[o'clock]
type/genre	noo3[2anwee3]
ugly	bishi3[iin]
under/below	ta7t
understand	bifham[fhimt]
university	jeem3a[at]
usually	3aadatan
vegetables	khiDra
verb	fi3l[2af3aal]
very/a lot/much	ktiir[adv]
view	manZar[manaaZir]
village	Day3a[Diya3]
vision	naZar
visit	bzuur[zirt]
visitor	zeeyir[zuwwaar]
vowel	7arf mit7arrik
wait	binTur[naTart]
waiter	(ya m3allim[if calling him]) / rrijeel / lgarsoon[eet]
waitress	(ya sitt[if calling her])/lmara
wake up	bfii2[fi2t]
walk	bimshe[mshiit]
want [wanted]	badde[keen badde]
washing machine	ghisseele[et]
waste/lose	bDayyi3[Dayya3t]
watch [TV]	bitfarraj[tfarrajt] 3a

GLOSSARY: ENGLISH - LEBANESE

English	Lebanese
we (are)	ni7na
wear	bilbus [lbist]
weather	Ta2s
Wednesday	l2irb3a
week	2usbuu3 [2asabii3]
weekend	niheeyit l2usbuu3
welcome [into one's home]	2ahlan [inv.]
welcome [response to shukran]	3afwan [inv.]
what do you think?	shu 2awlak/ ra2yak?
what?	shu?
what's wrong?	shu beek[e\un]?
when [in a statement]	lamma
when? [in a question]	2imtiin?
whenever/every time	killma
where from?	min ween?
where to?	la ween?
where?	ween?
wherever	weenma [+ verb]
which/that	yalle [in a statement]
which?	2ayya? [in a question]
while [a]	midde [et]
white	2abyaD [bayDa\biiD]
why?	leesh?
will [+ vb (future)]	ra7
wind [nn]	hawa
window	shibbeek [shbebiik]
wine	nbiid
winter	shshite
wish [I/we you a speedy recovery]	saleemtak
with	ma3
without	bala/ biduun
woman	mara [nisween]
wonder	bitsee2al [tsee2alt]
word	kilme [kalimeet]
work [nn]	shighil [2ashghaal]
work of art	3amal [2a3meel] fanne [iyye]
work [vb]	bishtighil [shtaghalt]
world	3aalam [3aweelim]
worry/be afraid	bkhaaf [khift]
would you like? [(used by person offering service)]	bitriid [e\o]?
write	biktub [katabt]
year	sine [sniin]
yellow	2aSfar [Safra\Sifr]
yes [familiar]	2e
yes [polite]	na3am
yesterday	mbeeri7
yet	ba3d
you [respectful]	7aDirtak [ik\kun]
you [f]	2inte
you [m]	2inta
you [p]	2into

INDEX

address 4
    finding an address 4
adjectives[describing words] 2,9
    comparative[comparing two things] 12
    feminine ending   **e**[after non-guttural letter] 2,9
                        a[after guttural letter] 2,9
    masculine, feminine[e/a] plural[iin] 2,6
    nationality mfp[e\iyye\iyye] 3
    plural of things = feminine singular[e/a] 6,9
    plural of people:
        regular[iin] 9
        irregular[eg kbaar...] 9
        aa with words containing **S, D, T, Z** 9
            with **r** 9
    superlative[comparing many] 12
        position 12
adverb[describes verb]+**ma**+verb [eg 2abil**ma** + vb] 15
adverbs of place 11
arab world geography 3
article[a/the/is/'s] 7
cities 4
clothes 14
colours 14
countries 4
courting 4
date 10
days of the week 10
directions 11
double consonant in the middle of a word 13
dual[een] 6
eating etiquette 7
electrical appliances 14
electronic gadgets 14
family 6
family relations 6
feeling[I'm] 2
film genre 15
food and drink, cafe 7
food and drink, restaurant 13
furniture 14
greetings 1
groceries 14
health care 9
hijri year 10
hobbies 15
hotel accommodation 12
lebanese pastimes 15
meeza 13
months of the year 10
names 1
nationality 3
negation[saying no/not]
    all tenses 9
    future 9
    imperative 7
    nouns and adjectives 4,5
    past 8
    present 5,7
nouns[naming words]
    feminine ending[a/e] 3
    people: masc, fem[e/a], pl[iin] 5,7
    plural of things 7

numbers
    + noun 6
    cardinal[1,2,3...] 4
    ordinal[1st, 2nd, 3rd...] 14
occupations 5
past activities 8
personal closeness 2
phone number 4
places around town 11
polite requests[3mool ma3ruuf / ...] 7
pronouns[2ana, ni7na, ...] 1
    demonstratives[hayda/hayde/haydool] 4,5
    formal[7aDirtak] 1
    object pronouns: me/us|you[mf p]| him/her/them 11
    object pronoun [yyee/yyeeha/yyeehun] after pronominal suffix 12
pronunciation
    ay > ee 13
    consonant cluster **i** 1,5,7
    feminine ending a/e as **t** / **it** 4,7,13
    two long syllables in succession 2
restaurant courses 13
root derivations[3-consonant root] 16
seasons 10
shopping places 14
suffixes[appended to end of words] 1
    after **l**[to/for] 14
    pronominal[ak\ik\kun....] 1
        appended to verb that ends in a consonant 11
        appended to verb that ends in a vowel 11
    possessive[my/our/your...] appended to   masc. noun 1
                                              fem. noun 4
taste 15
time 10
time expressions 10
tourism 16
transport[means of] 11
verbs[doing words]
    conditional[2iza/law] 16
    future [ra7] 9
        future continuous[bkuun/ra7 kuun] 11
    imperative[order] 7
    participle: no action[seekin], mobility[raayi7], have[2eekil] 15
    passive[action done to sthg/sone]
        present: verbal[binjiri7], adjectival[majruu7] 15
        past: verbal[njara7t], adjectival[kint majruu7] 15
    past[did] 8
        3rd person: non-guttural   **ee**[sheef...] 8
                        guttural   **aa**[khaaf...] 8
    have done 15
    had done 15
    past activities 8
    past continuous[was doing] 11
    present[do/am doing] 5,7
        dropping:
            the prefix **b/m**[after auxiliary/to/adverbs of time] 7
                                    [after ra7] 7,9
            the short vowel when a suffix is added 5
        prefix **bi** vs **by** 7
        present contiuous[3am] 10
    verbs of expressing[b2uul/bi7ke] 13
weather 16
working hours 5

www.ingramcontent.com/pod-product-compliance
Lightning Source LLC
Chambersburg PA
CBHW080811010526
44113CB00013B/2361